ELEVATE

MINDSET, MARKETING, AND HAPPINESS STRATEGIES FOR ALLIED HEALTH PRACTICE OWNERS

by
JILL WOODS & JONATHAN SMALL

JOIN US, WE'RE GOING UP

Many thanks to the team at Medi-Plinth for providing the plinth image for our cover. https://www.medi-plinth.co.uk/

ISBN: (paperback) 978-1-73928-311-7

Published by New Momentum Publishing

WE'RE HOLDING THE DOORS FOR YOU, JUMP IN

To Darren, Diane and Evan

For all the support you give,
so that we can help others

CONTENTS

PREFACE
by Tony Gavin

As a fellow healthcare practitioner, I am so excited to introduce you to "Elevate: Transforming Your Healthcare Business" by Jill and Jonathan. These two authors are not only colleagues, but also personal friends of mine, and I can confidently say that they are experts in the field of healthcare business.

Through my own experience and working with thousands of other private practitioners, I know that running a healthcare business can be challenging. It's not just about providing great care to patients, but also about growing and scaling your practice. That's why I wish this book was around when I first started my own practice.

In "Elevate," Jill and Jonathan share their combined wisdom and experience to help you take your healthcare business to the next level. The concept of "elevate" is not just about moving to a higher place, but also about promoting to a higher state and raising to a higher intellectual or spiritual level.

Jonathan Small, Tony Gavin, Jill Woods

What is important to note is that the authors understand the importance of running a successful healthcare business so that it can reach its full potential for patient care. By elevating your business, you will be better equipped to provide the best possible care to your patients, which is ultimately why our businesses exist.

The authors provide practical advice on how to gain momentum, release yourself from blocking your own progress, build a successful business, understand your worth as a healthcare professional, and navigate marketing and advertising in the digital age. They understand that your healthcare business can only grow as much as you do, and they are here to help you make that happen.

I highly recommend "Elevate" to any healthcare practitioner looking to take their business to the next level. It's a must-read for anyone looking to elevate both themselves and their business. Trust me, you won't regret it!

"I loved it. This book is for you if you want to take your business to the next level and attract the clients you want and have your well-being intact. It comes across in a holistic type of way, with your wellbeing and business interconnected. It's clear, directional, and fuelling, and a bit of reality hitting home which is a great kick start to get you moving and achieving all that you want to achieve. Definitely worthy of my bookshelf!"

Jessica van Dalfsen, Foot Health Practitioner, England

ABOUT US – THE AUTHORS

The universe brought Jill Woods and Jonathan Small together at a healthcare business conference (OSGO LIVE 2016), at which they had both been invited to speak. Unknown to each other apart from as fleeting names on social media, they found themselves speaking back-to-back at the conference. The content of their talks was similar, but the delivery of them was very different. Immediately, they both had the same thought: to collaborate on a book to help other healthcare business owners, bringing together their delivery styles to reinforce the valuable lessons and information they wanted to share. In the period of time since then, Jill and Jonathan have gotten to know each other well, so they will introduce each other to you.

Jonathan on Jill:

In my experience, it's rare to find people like me who have as much energy for what they do – people who would be happy doing it all for free, as they're so passionate about it. So when I saw Jill on stage at our first conference together, I immediately felt *this is someone like me*. She was so vivid, excited, and keen to share her wisdom. That brightness hasn't faded in all the time since then. As a Forces wife, Jill moved to the other side of the world early on in our co-authorship, but that hasn't diminished her keenness to get the job done. She is on a mission to help equip healthcare business owners so that they can better help their patients. Because of this, our paths have crossed many times outside of writing this book. Jill is the driving force behind so many great resources to help those clinic owners like myself, including the free-to-access Practice Momentum community and the National UK campaign #PodsHealHeels. Helping others runs through her bones, as demonstrated by the fantastic work she does supporting a leprosy charity in Nepal. The fulfilment and joy she gets from giving love in this way is so evident from the photos she shares.

Jill working with Nepal Leprosy Trust

Jill and I also have a shared interest in the outdoors and adventure, although due to geographical separation and a pandemic, the closest we have come to enjoying this together is when we met up in Kathmandu in 2017. Upon returning there from a trek to Everest Base Camp, some podiatry friends and I were drained emotionally and physically. We had all experienced challenges to our health. Then, we got just what the doctor ordered: a welcome and effective dose of Jill

Woods, who had travelled from the leprosy hospital to meet with us. I will always be grateful to her for making that journey. Her energy and love of life was infectious, and we were all soon feeling better because of our time with her.

Our shared journey into authorship has benefitted so much from Jill's energy, which drives the achievement of many amazing things. Whenever she shared the next section or chapter of the book with me, I could feel her passion in the words she had written, and I knew that our readers would sense it too. This is what I wanted to come across in the book: the passionate style of delivery at that first conference together. I believe we have achieved that, so that all the readers will benefit. It really has been an honour and pleasure not only to write this book with Jill, but also to count her as my friend.

Jill on Jonathan:

I'm a huge believer in serendipity and that things happen for a reason. It was one such occasion that caused my path and Jonathan's to cross, for which I will be forever grateful. Within five minutes of meeting, we decided to write a book – so obvious were our common ideas, values, and driving forces. Although, I have since discovered that we're also very different. Thankfully, Jonathan is more focused, ordered, and considered than me, which has brought this book into your hands. Realising that spontaneity isn't one of Jonathan's strongest powers, I'm so glad I caught him on a good day, and he agreed to co-authoring this book.

Jonathan and I share a strong passion for helping health professionals who are struggling, and that has been the glue in our collaboration. We both came at this project with the aim of helping as many practice owners as possible access our ideas and benefit from our experience, so that they can achieve more with their practices and lives. We both believe in combining a positive mindset and personal values with numbers-based decisions to build a successful practice. Using these principles, Jonathan has turned a tiny provincial podiatry practice into a powerhouse of profitability, serving an ever-growing community of patients. He is succeeding where many are struggling.

Taking what he has learnt in business, Jonathan has created a set of systems and processes he calls "Working Smarter not Harder." He now shares this with as many practitioners as will listen, in the hope of helping them build a better practice and more fulfilled life.

Jonathan loving his challenges

Away from work, Jonathan's life is focussed around family and fun, and he is a man who loves a challenge. Making it onto a British dragon boat team and to Everest basecamp are testaments to his tenacity and courage to push himself out of his comfort zone. One of the biggest challenges I've seen him conquer is public speaking. From the first time I saw him on stage, awkwardly struggling to speak and reading verbatim from sheets of notes, to now standing easily regaling people with his story and very confidently sharing his beliefs and ideas – it's like seeing a caterpillar transform into a butterfly. You will benefit from that transformation – as he shares his personal growth and what he has proved works in private practice.

As a team, our combined strengths have got this book over the finish line; but without him, my jumbled ideas would never have ended up in print. He's the driving force behind what you'll learn in this book, and for that I will always be very grateful.

If you would like access to us and our various resources, visit our website **www.elevatetools.com**

ABOUT YOU – THE READER

Firstly thank you for showing an interest in reading our book. When we originally planned it, we just wanted to bring together our combined knowledge and experience for those who may benefit from it. We thought that would be healthcare business owners who were encountering difficulties and asking themselves questions such as:

- How do I find energy to develop my business?
- How do I let go of the fears I have about growing my business?
- How do I engage with the process of change to create success?
- How do I value what my business does to ensure it is profitable?
- What action do I need to be taking to market my business better?
- How do I transform my business to be successful?
- How do I keep the success going and maintain my happiness?

We soon realised that those questions applied to any business owner, but equally they could apply to those with responsibility for the success of any business. In the area we focus on – healthcare – that could mean practice managers and lead clinicians as well as practice owners. So this book will be helpful to anyone who questions if they can achieve more for themselves, their clients (or patients) and their businesses, especially for those in allied healthcare.

Therefore you will notice that the text is written as if speaking to business owner directly. As Jill and Jonathan are both business owners, they frequently include themselves in the narrative and are referred to in the first person. Indeed Jonathan still owns his own healthcare practice and works in it as Lead Podiatrist, seeing patients himself each week. Both Jill and Jonathan can readily relate to all practice owners and the challenges they face on a day-to-day basis. So this book is focussed on helping you elevate your healthcare practice by delivering mindset, marketing and happiness for allied health practice owners.

INTRODUCTION

As healthcare providers with a combined fifty-five-plus years of experience, we've spent many years working in or with healthcare businesses around the world. Based on our lessons learned – both positive and negative – we feel a strong calling to help others transform themselves and their practices. We strongly believe that your healthcare business can only grow as much as you do – and we're here to help you make that happen. So *well done* for taking the first step by investing in this book to help you and your business grow!

In 2016, we – Jill and Jonathan – met at a podiatry business conference where we were both presenting. We clicked, deciding there and then that we should write a book in order to reach and help many more practitioners than we could individually. Jill had worked as both a podiatrist and a university podiatry lecturer, as well as a healthcare business mentor and marketeer. Jonathan had worked as a diabetes specialist podiatrist, a gait and movement analyst, and a consulting podiatrist for Offender Health – developing a "work smarter, not harder" approach to his thirty-plus years in private practice.

So, this book is the result of that collaboration, culminating from our combined wisdom, experience, and hard work in understanding how to elevate ourselves as healthcare business owners from *where you in your healthcare practice journey* to *where we want to be*. Note that use of the term *"we"* applies both to ourselves and our businesses throughout the book.

The word ELEVATE – which is the model of this book – is defined as:
- to move or raise to a higher place or position; lift up
- to raise to a higher state, rank, or office; exalt; promote
- to raise to a higher intellectual or spiritual level
- to raise the spirits; put in high spirits
- to raise (the voice) in pitch or volume

Just like an *elevator* moves between floors of a building, we've included seven floors (chapters) in this book to help you through the process of *elevating* yourself and your business. Each one can be completed on its own, and some key learning points are re-iterated on different floors. However we feel you'll get the most out of the book by starting at the first floor and working your way up a floor at a time, until you reach the top floor.

By the time you complete the book – combining the information from the whole journey for maximum effect – we hope you can bring your "dream practice" to life more quickly and effectively. Our ultimate aim is to equip you in better serving your patients, without sacrificing your own wants and needs.

Within each floor (chapter), you'll find similar features, including:

- Key learning points – look out for this symbol
- Content text with highlighted points and relevant quotes
- "Ask the Author" sections, where Jill or Jonathan will respond to key questions
- Exercises and activities for you to complete to help your transformation
- Action points to help ensure your progress

One key point to remember is that this book isn't called *Jack and the Beanstalk*. Growth doesn't just happen overnight, nor will you be able to climb a giant vine tomorrow to reach your ultimate destination. Instead, we are providing the ELEVATE seeds for you to plant and nurture – in your own way, for your own development. They will need regular attention and nutrition to thrive – ultimately helping your business grow. We hope you'll return to this book again and again on your transformative journey, so that the seeds we provide can grow as big and strong as possible.

Now it's time for you to explore the floors. Start at the ground floor, or take a ride in the elevator to a floor that interests you. Then, just step into the information held within. When you've had enough of one floor, try another; you can always come back at any time to visit any floor. Our elevator is at your disposal. Use it to ELEVATE yourself and your business.

You can start at any floor and move through them in any order, but we recommend starting with the foundations at Floor 1 and progressing up the floors from 1 through to 7. This will ensure that you don't miss a trick to help you on your ride in our elevator.

FLOOR 1 – ENERGISE

Helping You Gain Momentum

√ Your thoughts are important

√ Have a vision

√ Be the person who has achieved

√ Take responsibility

√ Consistency and discipline matter

√ Achieve momentum by doing

We're presuming that you're reading this book because you're a healthcare practice owner or manager, and you feel you are not where you want to be with your business. In short, you want change. You want different results for yourself and your practice. Yes? Fantastic! Then you're in the right place.

We could just give you a big list of all the tactics and tools you need to rejuvenate your practice and propel yourself to the next level. But years of doing this work has taught us something crucial: the factor that trips people up, time and time again, and defeats their efforts to get great results is *themselves*.

We've both seen just how important *you* are as the key element that creates transformation in your practice. Your thoughts, beliefs, habits, and actions all dictate where you will land. We've both seen this play out over and over again in practices around the world.

Achieving different results requires you to do different things – and do things differently. Initiating these changes requires you to gain new knowledge and implement it in a different way. So, on this first floor, we'll unpack the process of working on your business. In doing so, we hope to help you develop a different perspective, clearer goals, and more discipline than ever – to achieve those goals that have eluded you. In the process, we aim to energise you as you create momentum in your practice.

CREATING PRACTICE MOMENTUM

Creating momentum requires energy. Specifically, it requires *kinetic energy*, the definition of which is: "energy which a body possesses by virtue of being in motion." So, if we need to be in motion to experience kinetic energy and create that important momentum, how do we get into motion in the first place? We do so by tapping into the other form of energy, *potential energy*, which is defined as: "the energy possessed by a body by virtue of its position relative to others, stresses within itself, electric charge, and other factors."

In life and in your practice, what is the potential energy that will launch you into motion? It's simple: your thoughts!

Everything in our manmade world is a result of thought: the chair you're sitting on, the car you drive, the charity you give to that supports homeless people, the shop you buy your groceries in, and the shelves those groceries are stacked on. Everything is created or put into motion by a thought: an initiating, single thought.

To get your practice into motion and create your own momentum that takes you in the right direction, you first need to get really clear on a couple of things. That is, you must examine your thoughts around *what you believe is possible* and *what you want for your business.*

Your potential energy will come from your thoughts about the future of your practice, which includes your vision or dream – the picture in your mind of what you want to create. Your vision is the fuel for your momentum. So, our first question to you is:

WHAT IS YOUR VISION FOR YOUR PRACTICE AND YOUR LIFE?

It's a question we ask a lot of health practitioners, and we're constantly astounded at the number of professionals who either say, "I don't really have one," or they waffle a few ideas quickly, off the top of their heads, to make us believe they have one (we see you!). Most have no clear vision or goals planned for their businesses. Yet every day, they get up and get busy investing their time, energy, and money into a variety of activities that they hope will move the needle forward on their businesses. To our minds, that's madness. You're busting a gut – using up precious time, energy, money, and headspace – going in no particular direction. As evidence of this, we hear many practitioners saying, "I'm not really sure how I ended up here." They're operating on autopilot and not intentionally creating the businesses they want.

Getting clear on your business and life vision (we believe they're interrelated) can be one of the best things you'll ever do to improve your productivity and create momentum. So, before we get you into motion and a state of kinetic flow, let's first look at how to create a clear vision. As you're the person driving the development of the practice, let's start by getting real on *where you really are*, and *how you're operating*.

HOW ARE YOU ENGAGING IN LIFE ITSELF?

EXERCISE 1
A Quick Clarity and Reality Exercise

Take a clean page or piece of paper and write down your 100 percent honest answers to the following questions. Note: if you lie or smudge the truth, you're only undermining your own progress.

1. What personal habits (both constructive and destructive) do you practice every day, both in and away from the practice? (eg checking social media, doing exercise, drinking caffeine, reading)
2. What single habit do you feel is the most destructive?
3. What single habit do you feel is the most constructive?
4. If we used a drone with a camera to follow you for the whole day and watch what you do, what would you change? What would you *not* want us to see about your current habits or daily routine?

5. What is the thing you do every day that wastes the most time?
6. On a scale of 0–10 (with 0 being the worst), how would you grade your following behaviours at work:
   - Being totally clear on what you want to achieve
   - Taking full responsibility for the current state of your business
   - Being committed to developing your business
   - Being disciplined about doing what needs to be done every day
7. What will your life look like in five years' time if you keep living and working as you are in this moment?
8. What activities in your daily routine energise you?
9. What activities in your daily routine deplete you?
10. If you were totally fearless, what would you change tomorrow in your life?
11. What do you want your life to look like twelve months from now, both professionally and personally? (Take time to answer this question fully and honestly.)
12. Do you want to create change in your current life? If so, how?
13. On a scale of 0 to 10, how committed are you to creating change and new results for yourself and your business? Does your commitment level extend to an action as tenacious as spending two hours trying to pick up the pennies at the bottom of a wishing well using only a stick and old piece of chewing gum? That's full-on committed! (Can anyone reassure Jill it wasn't just her doing that as an eight-year-old?!)

Now look back over your answers. What do you think you'll need to change about how you currently do things, in order to achieve your desired results? There's a great saying:

"How you do anything is how you do everything."
(Van Kleeck 1999)

What are your honest answers telling you about how you're engaging currently in life and business? Are you satisfied with your answers? Will the gain for you be worth the act of fully committing to make big changes?

YOUR LIFE VISION MATTERS

If at this point, you're rolling your eyes in a kind of *"really?"* motion, or you're tempted to flick to find the start of the next floor, we just want to remind you of the point we made at the start. You bought this book or picked it up to read because you're looking for different results in your business.

<blockquote>Different results require different actions.</blockquote>

If you've never taken the time to develop a clear vision for your life (which includes your business), we suggest that's the first thing you must do. Doing so will help you achieve those new results that could impact your life in so many ways. Still with us? Great! Let's do this….

In his now world-famous book *The 7 Habits of Highly Effective People*, Stephen Covey sights the second all important habit as *start with the end in mind* (Covey 1989). So, when we're starting out and looking to drive change in our lives and practices, we must first get really clear on what our destination looks like. We appreciate that your picture will change over time, but you must start somewhere with your first vision of your whole life.

THE WORD DOESN'T MATTER

We like to use the term *vision* because it feels exciting and full of possibilities, but whether you prefer to talk about your vision, dream, or big picture doesn't matter. Ultimately, we're talking about the same thing: achieving the things we most want in life. Call them what you will!

Be under no illusion! Achieving anything requires effort – not always as much as people think, but effort nonetheless.

What matters most is the energy and the intention that sits behind the words you choose and goals you want to achieve. Having a clear motivating vision/dream/big picture will drive you out of bed on the tough days. It will keep you moving when your entire team resign, or on the days when the cashflow is dwindling and you can't see a way forward.

You need a vision to motivate you, inspire you, and excite you. Positive energy will play a big part in your success journey, so start with a vision for something that makes you feel – yes really feel – excited. Having positive energy behind your *what* and *why* will make a difference when the tough days roll in, and you must dig deep to keep going. Having positive intentions and high energy behind your vision is crucial. So, let's start by getting really clear on your vision:

- What is it that you really want for your life?
- Can you picture it?
- Can you talk about it in detail?
- What are you aiming for?
- Where are you going?
- What do you want to achieve?
- What does success look like for you?
- How will it feel when you get there?

These kinds of questions will start getting you clearer on your vision – for both your life and practice. Or at the very least, they will help you realise how little intentional thought you've given to your optimal direction and destination. Often, people are limited in their thinking when it comes to developing their vision, because they work from a position of circumstance. That is, they look around themselves – at their business and other similar businesses – and use that information as a benchmark against which to measure their probable progress.

We want to encourage you to build your vision based on *possibility*, not just based on your *current reality*. What is *actually* possible for you? Really possible? Remember the old adage: aim for the stars, and you'll at least hit the moon? People who create great things do so from a position of wondering what is possible, not predicting what is likely. Don't limit your future options by thinking small and safe.

We live in a time of technology, scientific advances, and personal freedoms that enable seemingly endless possibilities. So why stifle your vision for your life and settle for mediocrity? If you're struggling to see beyond the "look-alike" practice down the road, take two minutes to find evidence that different and greater things are possible. Is it true that individuals with a single thought have disrupted well-established industries and gone on to help thousands of people with their innovative product or service? Yes, of course it's true.

So, can you find existing evidence to debunk the thoughts that could very well be holding you back? Here are some questions you might ask, finding evidence to support your answers:

- Do people over the age of fifty-five build thriving healthcare practices?
- Is it possible to create a seven-figure healthcare practice?
- Can practice owners have a great quality of life, even while running a thriving business?
- Is it possible to specialise in supporting a small niche group of patients and still build a thriving business?
- Have people created thriving practices in rural locations?

Whatever thoughts are holding you back, look for evidence that those thoughts aren't true. When it comes to running a successful healthcare practice within a specific set of criteria, if one person can do it, so can you. As long as the ideas you look for are aligned with your values and genuine desires, they can add real fuel to your vision-building.

OK, pep talk over! Let's dig in.

CREATING YOUR VISION

Clearly seeing in your mind's eye what you want to achieve will help you stay motivated, able to articulate your vision to those around you (which is important if you want their help), and on track to achieving it.

You must structure your vision so that it's super clear, motivating to you, and informing of the actions you must take to get there.

We've defined eleven distinct areas where your performance can impact how you experience and enjoy life. It's possible to work on your behaviour in – and experience of – all of these categories in order to create a life that you'll love. They are:

1. **Health and Fitness** – how well you feel and how well you can move
2. **Intellectual Life** – your thoughts, interests, and beliefs
3. **Emotional Life** – your behaviour and reactions to situations
4. **Character** – your personality traits
5. **Spiritual Life** – this can be religion or a sense of connection to something bigger than yourself
6. **Love Life** – intimate and close relationship with a long-term partner
7. **Social Life** – relationships with people close to you
8. **Parental Life** – your role as parent, guardian, or supporter of the next generation

9. **Financial Life** – your money picture
10. **Career** – employment or entrepreneurship
11. **Quality of Your Life** – things you want in your life

Not many people are so intentional as to break life down like this – and dedicate time to creating a vision and roadmap for improving all these elements. We'll leave it up to you to decide if that's a path you want to go down. For now, we just want you to be aware of these elements of your life and the impact they can have on your experience as you start creating your vision. For the purpose of this book, we'll focus simply on the *career* category, as that's where being a business owner or manager sits.

As best as you can, ignore the voices trying to talk you out of this change. Silence them by intentionally thinking about the change of plans that got you to this place of wanting to pursue a new or refined vision. Remember, life often trains us to operate and achieve well below what is actually possible for us as human beings. You don't need to settle for what life serves you. You can actively participate in creating your vision. Be as bold as you dare. Create your vision not from your current reality or circumstances, but from what is possible, even if it currently seems impossible. You can have it all!

People are held back by the worries of:

- *I'm not ready yet.*
- *I'm not qualified enough.*
- *I'm too young/old.*
- *I'm too far behind.*
- *People will judge me negatively.*

Yet there are thousands of examples we could cite where the underdog won, where seemingly insurmountable odds were beaten, or where someone came from nowhere to succeed. So, try not to play small and have your dreams dampened by potential limitations.

Finally, it's not your job to worry about the minutia of how the heck you're going to do this at this moment. Become 100 percent focused on *what you want your life to be* without worrying about *how on earth you will make this your reality.* If you're serious about creating your vision, you'll dedicate a good chunk of time (we'd suggest at least a week or more, on and off) to considering the question:

What do you really want?

After all, we're talking about the rest of your life here. You're not just deciding what you'd like for supper! What do you want in the eleven key areas of your life? You might not want to change the world. (We do, which is why we're writing this book – and there's nothing to be coy about if that's what you truly want.) But if you didn't want to change something about your practice, it's unlikely you'd be taking the time to read this book. This is your time. Are you ready to take the next BIG step? Pretty much anything is possible if you desire it enough.

EXERCISE 2
Vision building

- Go somewhere quiet.
- Go somewhere you won't be disturbed.
- Go somewhere you'll feel relaxed and safe.
- Go and vision build.

Write everything down that's currently floating around in your head relating to the future of your practice. Your ideas, your fears, your passions, your secret wishes, how all of this makes you feel – just keep writing – random ideas, snap images, pages and pages. Keep writing until you're done.

Now that you've got all of that in your conscious mind, take a few clean sheets of paper and write out your perfect day, five years from now. Write it in the present tense and make it as descriptive and real as possible. What would your perfect day really look like?

Note: This isn't a goal-setting exercise; this is a vision-building practice. We aren't looking for a few bullet points, but an exciting full picture of what your future is going to look like. You're putting thoughts into words and painting the big picture. Also, this isn't a more, better, different type of exercise – this is thinking BIG and expansively. Ask yourself:

- *What do I believe about my practice?* – Describe new, empowering beliefs.
- *What do I want in my practice?* – Dream from possibility, not your current reality.
- *Why do I want it?* – Think about the impact will it have on myself and other people?
- *How will I feel when I have accomplished it?* – Emotion is a powerful motivator.

Spend some time reworking your dream day. Re-read your description, then re-write it. Create something that, when read, evokes real emotions in you – excitement, pride, joy, etc.

Your follow-up task is to revisit that dream day as often as possible. It is a well-known fact that your subconscious doesn't know the difference between current 3D reality and imagined reality. That repetition of a message to your subconscious mind will help steer your actions and habits, which will, over time, steer you towards achieving your vision. So when it comes to your vision, read it, hear it, see it, smell it, and feel it every day if you can. Each day is moving you closer to success.

BE-DO-HAVE

So, you've got your vision squared away, and you've practiced the thoughts that will fuel your kinetic energy. Now let's get busy bringing it to life to get what you want!

The first concept in implementing your vision is something that we're guessing you won't be expecting, because we won't initially walk you through how to set goals, plan your days, or monitor your weekly progress. Instead, we'll take a step further back from that and start with addressing who you are as a person. This is a piece of the puzzle that virtually all practitioners are missing, as they set out to work towards their vision. We must address *you and the person you are*, because that will dictate the actions you take and ultimately the results you get. Let us explain.

Many people come at life from this model:

Have → Do → Be.

In other words, they tell themselves that once they have the thing, for example a thriving practice, then they'll be able to do things like take a long holiday – and then they will be successful. They're waiting for the time to be right, so they can achieve the thing they're envisioning. For example: When I have forty new patients every week, then I'll pay for a bookkeeper to help me with my accounts. And then I'll be freer to work on my marketing and grow the business. Or: Once I have all the information and qualifications I need, then I will get good at marketing to attract more high-paying patients. And then I will be more wealthy and able to pay for a cleaner and marketing person.

It's a story we hear over and over again. But it will never pan out like that, because if we're always waiting for our circumstances to change first and are set on not taking action (the *doing* part) until our circumstances change, nothing changes. We will just repeat our story and cycle of achievements – or lack of them – over and over again.

How long will you wait for the timing to be just right – or for you to have enough time, money, resources, qualifications, or permission – to do the thing you're putting off? Will you ever actually have the exact thing you're waiting for before you take action? NO!

When we stall and don't take any action, we don't get the results we say we want. Instead, we stay in the *have* phase – hoping and wishing and waiting for something that will probably never come. We can only hope that we'll end up in a position that makes us feel happy, successful, or wealthy. In short, the Have-Do-Be model doesn't work. So instead, we need to flip the model. What has been shown time and time again to work is:

Be → Do → Have.

Let's explain this one:

Be – Getting the results you want requires being a certain way as a person. The person you are heavily influences the results you get. Are you a vision-driven, committed action-taker or a hesitant person fearful of risks and change? Being the latter person will never get you the results you want. You must be the person who will change your life's course, if you want to step into your vision.

Do – Take the right, consistent actions with commitment and discipline. Once you know who you need to be, then it's time to do what is needed.

Have – Being the right kind of person and taking the right consistent action will lead you to have the life you envisioned.

So, once you have your vision mapped out, you next must understand who the person is that you need to be, in order to achieve that vision. Many people rant online about taking massive action, knuckling down, and hustling hard. But flogging yourself into doing, before you have addressed the person you're being, will lead to friction, because the actions won't be aligned with the type of person you are.

We see this *all* the time. We've taught thousands of practitioners the things they must *do* to make their practice marketing effective (the doing part). But because they're not *being* the people who believe in having a successful, specialist, rural practice, for example, they just don't put half of what we have taught them into action. They procrastinate and consistently self-sabotage their progress by making excuses or finding other work to get busy on.

It's not their fault; they're just missing this piece of the puzzle. They aren't being and acting like the person who will create an awesome, thriving, specialist, rural practice. If you don't address this state of being and doing, you'll end up really pushing against your own natural resistance, possibly burning yourself out, and only moving the needle forward a tiny bit – quite possibly getting similar results to the ones you've always seen. Or sometimes, you'll charge ahead using brute force and make progress, only to stall from exhaustion and start going backwards – ending up close to where you started off or worse.

Ask anyone who has achieved anything significant in their life: were they the same person taking the same actions before they started their journey, and at the end of their journey? We're pretty sure that every single one of them would tell you no, they were a very different person by the end. They had to change the person they were being in order to start doing things differently, so that they could progress towards their goals and get different results.

The person you are is the sum total of your thoughts, beliefs, attitudes, emotions, and actions. So you've made a start, because we've already helped you become clear on your thoughts about the future of your practice, in the form of your vision. Next, we need to address your beliefs, attitudes, emotions, and actions. All four are very closely connected.

What you believe and feel about your chances of success, and the attitude you have, will greatly influence your day-to-day actions.

Learning the required actions to achieve your vision is only part of the puzzle, as we have explained. It's how you carry out those actions that will influence your results. It's applying the right commitment, energy, discipline, and consistency to those actions that will bring your vision alive.

If you educate yourself and learn what actions to take – and then become a person committed and disciplined to taking those new actions consistently – you'll start seeing different results. That evidence of progress will reinforce that you're doing a great job, and the right actions will become less of an effort and more habitual.

So, who are you being in this moment? Are you being the person who:

- Has a clear vision of what you want to create?
- Sets quarterly business goals?
- Sets clear objectives each day?
- Takes ownership of the situation and responsibility no matter the circumstances?
- Sets boundaries and sticks to them?
- Has an accountability partner that you keep in touch with every week?

Or are you being the person who:

- Is just doing the next thing without thinking where it's taking you?
- Has no clear goals and lurches from one idea to another?
- Is busy being busy, but not always moving forward?
- Makes excuses for not getting things done and blames other people and circumstances?
- Lets other people force their will and wants onto you at the expense of your own?

Because that's not the kind of person who will achieve their business goals anywhere nearly as quickly as someone who acts like they're already successful in achieving those goals. Deciding on the kind of person to be provides you with a filter through which to pass all of your decision-making from this point onwards. Then you can simply ask yourself:

What would someone who has already achieved (insert your goal here) do in this situation?

Say, for example, Jonathan's business goal for this quarter is to attract 150 new patients with a few key pathologies that his practice would love to see more of. When his alarm goes off early in the morning to do some planning before work, would someone who has already achieved their business goals hit snooze? Or would they get their backside out of bed, pull on their clothes (set out the night before), grab a coffee, and head for a quiet spot with a notepad – knowing that this is the best time to brain-dump some ideas before considering an alternative course of action?

When Jonathan is at work and a patient doesn't show up, and he's really tempted to reach for his phone and scroll his friends' social media profiles, this is another good time for him to ask himself: *What would someone who has smashed their business goals be doing in this situation?* Hint: They wouldn't be reaching for their phone!

You must start *being* the person who has already achieved the thing you desire, so that you'll take the appropriate action to get your desired results. We'll say that again, because it's so important, we want to make sure you heard us. You must start BEING the person who has already achieved the thing you desire, so that you'll take the appropriate action to get your desired results.

The really exciting bit about this is that you actually get to choose. Every moment of every day, you get to choose how you show up, who you're operating as, and what actions you're taking. You must start asking yourself: *Who do I need to be to achieve the goal I have set myself?* Then, going forward every day, choose to be the version of yourself who will achieve the goal you've set. In your business, will you be the business leader? The CEO of your practice? The person making the right choices and taking the actions that get you the desired end results?

We're really hoping that this is making sense, because this is one of the key factors that will make the difference between being successful or struggling both professionally and personally.

THREE VITAL CHARACTERISTICS FOR SUCCESS

The person you must be in order to succeed is based on key personal traits. We guarantee that these will always include: taking responsibility for your life, committing to doing what it takes to achieve your vision, and being disciplined enough to show up day after day, even when the next-door neighbour's house alarm keeps you awake half the night. Through everything, you will succeed if you keep showing up – committed to achieving your vision and taking full responsibility for the situation you find yourself in each day. To start creating momentum, you will need to be responsible, committed, and disciplined to start showing up in a new way.

TAKE RESPONSIBILITY

Take 100 percent responsibility for where you are now in your business, and you'll become empowered to change your situation. If you don't take responsibility, you instead adopt a *victim* approach. If you become the victim to a situation, you believe it's someone else's doing. If that's really the case, you don't have the power to undo the situation. For example, if you have a sudden dip in new patient numbers, and you decide to blame the poor economy or the fact a new practice has opened up down the road, there's absolutely nothing you can do to change either of those things. You become a victim of circumstance. If you believe life just happens to you, you're powerless to make any changes or achieve different results, because it's totally out of your control.

> The more responsibility you can take for each of the situations you find yourself in, the more power you give yourself to change your circumstances.

From a victim's perspective, any lack of success is often someone else's fault – or the economy's, or the poor local demographic's, or the weather's.

Does any of this resonate with you? Do you remember a time when you've pointed the finger at someone else or a situation external to you, and blamed that factor for a problem in your practice? If you take responsibility for your situation, you can change it – and therefore change its outcome. So, if you do see a sudden drop-off in new patient numbers, instead of pointing the finger at something you can't control, reframe the situation by asking yourself:

> What can I do to change this situation?

That very simple question puts you back in control. You're responsible for what you think, everything you do, and how you respond to every situation. You're also responsible for how you feel about the situation! Embrace that responsibility and find yourself on the road to achieving your vision.

Dear Jonathan – Have you always taken steps in the right direction for you and your business?

> *In short, the answer to this is a definite "no." I have many examples of steps which I thought were in the right direction for both my businesses and myself, but they*

turned out to take me completely opposite to where I needed to go. One of the common patterns for me occurs during decisions I make based on cost rather than need. While I have a great eye for bargains, my curiosity over new products tends to lead me down the proverbial garden path, buying things for my business that don't fit with my plans or goals. In fact, some of my purchase decisions even hinder me, slow me down from progressing, or stop me dead in my tracks. I have many clinical gadgets and toys that never see the light of day, but at least they could potentially be put to good use in the future. However, if I don't make use of them and can only sell them at a loss, then they were a mistake to buy in the first place.

One step I definitely took in the wrong direction for one of my businesses occurred more than twenty years ago, and the effects of that decision are still felt to this day. In the 1990s, I was working for the National Health Service (NHS) in the UK and regularly recommended a famous brand of foot file to my patients to better care for their own feet. This particular foot file was effectively designed and recommended by many chiropodists/podiatrists around the UK. Then one day, the manufacturers changed the design to something they believed was more aesthetically pleasing to increase their retail sales. The problem with the new design was that it reduced the file's effectiveness, suitability, and usability. I tried to get the manufacturer to reverse their decision on changing the design, but my request fell on deaf ears.

So I sourced a better foot file from one of my suppliers at the time, negotiated a bulk order discount, and started a business selling the foot file – initially to other local NHS patients. Basically, local NHS chiropodists/podiatrists would provide a mail-order slip to their patients to complete and send to us, with accompanying payment for the foot file. We would then post the item directly to the patients, and this was the start of Health First Foot Care Products.

This business model proved to be successful, and within a couple of years, we had grown from selling single foot files to a full range of more than fifty footcare products. Our order forms were being handed out in NHS podiatry departments around the UK. Our growth curve was exponential, and we were an early adopter of an online shopping site which I called www.firstaidforfeet. co.uk. We even gave back to the NHS departments through a commission scheme to help them fund new equipment to benefit their patients.

Then one day, a sales rep from one of our main trade suppliers came to visit my private podiatry clinic. He observed with interest what my staff were doing: processing and packing up orders for foot care products, ready for dispatch around the UK. He asked about our process, and I explained how it all worked. He then took one of our glossy, illustrated order forms back to his company headquarters, and six months later, a copycat service was being promoted by them. They even established an exact-same commission scheme for NHS referrers.

You can imagine how I felt at the time. Even though they'd been making money from me – as one of my suppliers of my mail order and online business – they saw a market opportunity to make more money for themselves by duplicating my business model. I was unable to compete on price (as they were supplying me), and as an established podiatry supplier, they had much more leverage with the NHS.

So I effectively gave up on this business model. I lost my passion for the innovative service I 'd set up, and I blamed that company for the demise of my service, due to their plagiaristic approach. I stopped actively promoting my business of distributing products to podiatry patients, and it rotted for many years.

Nowadays, the service my "competitor" set up is worth millions of pounds. Once it had become established, they quickly withdrew the commission scheme they'd copied from me, so the NHS referrers also lost out.

But now when I reflect on it, I realise that the problem was me, not my supplier. I allowed them to effectively bully me out of the marketplace, and I quit. I didn't adapt to survive. As a result, I took a step that said "no" to lots of other market possibilities (such as other retail avenues), instead of saying "yes." My choice not to fight back against my perceived failure, once competition arose, was most definitely a step in the wrong direction.

COMMITMENT

To make big changes in your life, you must really commit to them – with a *come hell or high-water* type of commitment. We're all committed to something in our lives; our ultimate success hinges on 'what'.

- Do you know 'what' you're committed to?
- 'What' you are really committed to?

Whatever you're committed to becomes your filter for decision-making. Ensure the thing you're committed to is something positive that you desire. Being committed involves more than just hot air or hollow words. It's a way of being. Your commitment isn't just a word you share hollowly to describe yourself, but it's reflected in your actions. It's backed by 3D evidence that you care more than anything about your success.

No one says, "I'm committed to being a smoker," or, "I'm committed to being lazy." Their daily actions just show what they are committed to. In fact, words often don't give us the real picture. How many people tell us they're on a diet, and then they sit eating doughnuts and telling us that they deserve a treat? What are they committed to? Losing weight or comfort eating?

Commitment means going all-in, no matter the cost. Be under no illusion: to achieve this new vision will take time and energy, and there's a price to pay. What are you prepared to sacrifice to create this new reality? The time, money, and energy must come from somewhere. Where will you get the extra you need? In pursuit of your vision:

- Are you prepared to get up at 5:30 a.m., stop watching TV during the week, and give up two nights out a week, or go to bed later?
- Are you prepared to cut back on other business costs, raise your prices, or sell more to cover the extra costs?
- Are you prepared to resign from your children's school's parent committees, stop being the football club treasurer, or hang up your stamp collection for a year or so to gain the extra energy and headspace you'll need?

Success always comes at a price. What price are you prepared to pay? How committed are you, really, to your vision?

A small commitment warning: Beware the danger of not keeping your commitment.

If you say you'll do something, and then you let others or yourself down and don't do what you promised, you'll teach both yourself and others that you're not trustworthy. This dishonesty with your promises puts you on a very slippery slope to low self-esteem. That kind of "commitment" to unreliability can very quickly become disempowering.

If you find yourself unable to follow through, it's very likely that old habits and patterns are controlling your actions, and you'll end up repeating them – until you commit to being a different person and doing things differently. Then, you'll shift your results. A great way to show your commitment is to share your vision with other people. Go public on what you plan to achieve. That will help build in accountability, something many people find helpful in staying committed to a vision.

DISCIPLINE

This is the third important personal trait. Possessing the discipline to show up day after day, week after week, month after month – and continuing to do the things you know are crucial to bring your vision to reality – are so important. Even on the days when you don't feel like it, when you're really tired and would much rather do something else, discipline can keep you moving.

Sporting champions don't win without the discipline to train hard, eat a restricted diet, and pass on anything resembling a social life, year after year. To succeed in business, you need a similar discipline.

Here's the sticking point: in business, no one is coming to save you. There's no business fairy godmother just over the hill.

It's your business, your vision, your team, and your life. You must be the driver of this particular bus, and to travel on the route you desire for your business and life, you'll need discipline to stay on course. Yes, there are people, courses, conferences, and books that can help you along the way, but as the old saying goes: *only you can do your push-ups.*

*Only **you** can create the vision for what you want to build.*
*Only **you** can decide on the culture you want to develop in your practice, and enforce that.*
*Only **you** can deliver authentic marketing content showing the real you, your beliefs, and values.*
*Only **you** can develop the services you want to, and are proud to, deliver.*

Ultimately, it's down to you to be disciplined enough to achieve the vision you've set for yourself. How disciplined are you? To be the person you must be to succeed, do you think you need to be more disciplined?

We've explored three of the most important character traits you need to demonstrate as the leader of your business. There are hundreds of other traits you may choose to embody, but these are the three that we feel are crucial to any successful business practice – or deep personal change. Once you embrace these, we encourage you to explore for yourself many of the other traits – like compassion, active listening, inclusivity, happiness, kindness, organisation, fun, thriftiness, and being systemised or driven.

MOMENTUM

We've created clarity on what you want, and the person you need to be, to achieve your vision. Now let's get started on creating that all-important momentum. You must start somewhere with putting your longer-term vision into action. We suggest that you start with enacting some short-term goals. They will help keep you focused and reduce your chances of drifting off your desired route.

How can you begin to formulate short-term goals, when your vision seems large and futuristic? To make progress, you must take the vision for your business and life and start to break it down. Instead of working from where you are towards where you want to be, we'll give you a structure that should improve your odds of success. If we stand where you are today and look out into the future to the vision you've designed, it can feel like a very long way away and a huge step up from where you are now. In short, it can be really demoralising or even seem impossible, so you may feel defeated before you've even begun.

Also, if you get up every morning and revisit your vision (which we highly recommend you do), and then pick one thing at random that could move you forward and try to start working towards that, there's a good chance you'll feel overwhelmed and start procrastinating and self-sabotaging your day. Without a clear plan and logical milestones along the way, you'll waste a lot of time, money, and energy – and will likely lose momentum and get demoralised. Keep your vision clear in your mind, but don't view it as one massive, insurmountable to-do list. We'll help you break it down into smaller chunks and move the horizon much closer.

THE MOMENTUM CREATING SYSTEM

We've already completed STEP 1 of the system: create a clear and exciting vision for your life and business. In this instance, you've created a vision for your business.

STEP 2: As humans, we're motivated by seeing progress. So we recommend you break your calendar down, going forward from today, into ninety-day increments. This has the impact of moving the finish line much closer to you than a twelve-month or two-year plan. A much closer deadline gives more urgency to the tasks you must do and makes success more likely, and progress timelier than if you were working towards a twelve-month deadline.

STEP 3: Go back to your vision for your business and put a timescale on each element of your vision – anything from one month to five years.

STEP 4: Now pull all the elements that have a time scale of one year or less into a new list. These are going to be your BIG overarching goals and your focus for the next twelve months. We'll call them your *foundation goals*.

STEP 5: From these foundation goals, at the start of every ninety-day or three-month block (or preferably just before), tease out five(ish) smaller goals which, once achieved, will move you towards your foundation goals. These are much smaller baby steps to move you forward – your ninety-day or quarterly goals.

STEP 6: Every Friday afternoon or Sunday evening, look at these ninety-day goals and tease out little projects from them that you can work on the following week to help you reach your quarterly goals.

STEP 7: Every workday evening before you close up for the night, look over your weekly projects and decide what tasks you'll have time to work on the following day to move yourself towards completing your weekly projects.

You can see that instead of getting into work on a Monday morning and looking at your vision for your business – trying to decide what to do that day to move yourself towards that vision (too big a jump) – we've systematically worked back from the vision, chunking down the work. So, when you get into work on Monday, Tuesday, Wednesday, Thursday, and Friday mornings, you already know what small tasks you must work on. They aren't massive. They aren't overwhelming, and they don't feel like a ridiculously big leap from where you are now.

Hopefully you can see how this simple system will help keep you really focused on what you must do every day to stay on track with your big vision – without feeling defeated before you've even begun.

During the ninety days ahead, there's no need to go back and look at your foundation goals. Your focus for the next ninety days is your ninety-day goals and nothing else – other than your regular admin and business practices, like treating patients. No other projects or bright ideas are allowed to creep onto your to-do list for those next ninety days. We would urge you to overestimate what you can achieve in your foundation goals, but underestimate what you can achieve in a quarter and each day. It's much better for morale to complete two tasks and be able to add extra tasks from your weekly projects than to have twenty-five things left undone at the end of the day. It takes a few weeks to get the hang of what's realistic in setting milestones, because there will always be problems – steps in the process you hadn't considered, or other more urgent tasks that must take priority.

Our advice would also be to just put something into motion. It doesn't need to be perfect. There's no need to second-guess what will happen. Action will get you in motion, even if it's super slowly towards your goal.

EXERCISE 3
Quarterly (Ninety-Day) Goal

We want you to identify one relatively short-term element from your business vision, that if you were to achieve, would provide you with indisputable proof that you're making progress and creating momentum in your practice. One simple-but-impactful goal can fuel your desire and willingness to get out of bed for the next ninety days, come hell or high water, and help you become the person who can hit that goal. That goal could be like the one we mentioned previously for Jonathan – to attract 150 new patients with a few key pathologies that his practice would love to see more of.

Next, it's time to write out this quarterly goal in a way that will be both motivating and achievable. Our suggestion would be to write it:

- In the present tense, like it has already happened.
- So it's positive and empowering – not "I will stop wasting time on social media" but "I will schedule thirty minutes a day to be proactive on social media."
- Using *I* or *we*, so you practice taking ownership.
- So it's very specific – making it really clear what you're wanting to achieve.
- So it's measurable – attaching a number or some sort of tangible outcome to it.
- So it's achievable – asking yourself: *Is there evidence this is achievable? Can I learn the skills/knowledge required?* Your mind must see and believe it's achievable

- In a way that it feels relevant – asking yourself: *What will be the impact of achieving this?* or *Why do I want this?*
- With a deadline date – ninety days from today.

There you have it: your first ninety-day or quarterly goal. You can repeat this for as many goals as you would like, but start with 1 or 2 to help ensure that they are achievable. Write your goals out on a piece of paper and share that with people close to you who won't mock your vision or pop your bubble. Give it to those who will be excited for you and encourage you over the next ninety days. Note: Business goals can be a mix of those set by you as the owner and some set through collaboration with your team members.

The big overriding goals like financial and growth targets for the business need to be driven by the owner or senior management team. But including other team members in lower-level goal-setting, like changes to clinical processes or ideas for improvements in efficiency, can be empowering and strengthen the team.

Now every Friday afternoon or Sunday evening, you're going to look at these ninety-day goals and tease out from them little projects you and your team can work on the following week to move yourself closer to your quarterly goals. Then every workday evening before you close up for the night, you'll ask each member of the team to look over the weekly projects and decide what tasks they'll have time to work on the following day to move you collectively towards completing your weekly projects.

There you have it! You now have the knowledge and the system to start creating all that important momentum in your practice. You'll be working intentionally towards your vision rather than cruising on autopilot, going who knows where.

ACTION POINTS TO ENSURE YOU ARE ENERGISED

☐ Set the foundations of what you really want

☐ Complete the clarity and reality exercise

☐ Create your vision for your life and business

☐ Complete the vision building exercise

☐ Make sure you take responsibility

☐ Commit to being committed

☐ Decide to be disciplined

☐ Complete the 90-day (quarterly) goal exercise

YOU'RE NOW ENERGISED √

NOTES

FLOOR 2 – LET GO:

Releasing You from Blocking Your Own Progress

- ✓ Our brains are neuroplastic.
- ✓ Going through pain brings some benefits.
- ✓ You must change.
- ✓ Learn to improve your well-being.
- ✓ Build and focus on your dream.
- ✓ Ignore the negative voices.

How many times have you heard a voice in your head saying, "You can't do that," or "It won't work," or "You're not good enough"? Maybe it isn't even just coming from you. It could be your friends, family, colleagues, or social network contacts saying such things to you, reinforcing the negative beliefs you already had running around your brain.

Now imagine that internal voice saying, "You can do that," or "It will work," or "You're good enough." You simultaneously hear those messages from others around you. It doesn't take much to start believing in yourself, the decisions you make, and the actions you take. However, it also doesn't take much to let the negative voices back in either. This flexibility in our thinking occurs because of neuroplasticity.

Neuroplasticity is our brain's ability to change continuously throughout our lives.

Fortunately, there are some great ways to help neuroplasticity work for our success rather than against it. But first we must consider why we need help with changing our brains (mindsets), and why overcoming mindset blocks is so important to our businesses. Understanding how your brain responds when interacting with others and making crucial decisions will help you run your practice more successfully.

Our childhood experiences lay the foundations for our fears, anxieties, behaviours, happiness, and confidence. These traits form directly as a result of who we interact with in our early years and the environment in which we're brought up. When we add in the genes that we inherit, it's no wonder that we're all different.

Through our teenage years, we develop our own mindset of how we approach the world, sometimes rebelling against those who don't appear to be in tune with us at the time, as all while expanding our type and number of "influencers." We start to listen to our peers more than our parents, as we find them comfortable to be around, enjoying shared activities and experiences. This process creates bonds that can make us feel more secure, accepted, and heard – all of which are important to our self-esteem.

However, those peers will have different mindsets to us – from their own childhood journeys – which will reflect upon, shape, and change our own thoughts/beliefs (and vice versa) as we grow. We trust what these influencers tell us, as we know them and (generally) like them. Depending on our personality, we may adopt their mindsets more than our own innate ones, and this can continue into our adult behaviours, with influence flowing both directions within our closest relationships.

This trust isn't usually based on some validated, scientifically-proven, hierarchical, emotional or intellectual intelligence quotient, but more on a simplistic, emotionally-driven need of our own. We possess a primal need to be wanted/needed, and we end up trusting those who fulfil those needs – if they do so consistently and authentically. We tend to trust their opinions, whether they have real knowledge and understanding to serve us or not.

How does this dynamic factor into running a healthcare practice? This relational process continues throughout adulthood and comes into play when starting or running our healthcare businesses. We may ask our nearest and dearest, "What should I call my business?" or "What do you think of my new logo?" or "Should I move the location of my business to…?" They may not have any specialist business knowledge or understanding, and they may not even end up as our customers. Yet we choose to trust them with our important decisions, since we trust and know them as individuals – and as our influencers.

Now contrast that with when you need help to treat a patient's condition that you may not have come across before, or one that isn't responding to your usual treatments. Would you ask those same people, who may have no specialised healthcare knowledge or understanding? It's more likely you would approach someone who has proven credibility in the field for which you're seeking help. Yet you may still be influenced by whether you know or like that person, as to whether you trust what they're telling you.

The basis for obtaining scientific proof is to remove that subjective, emotional, "human" bias from our decision-making. But we don't seem to use such scientific processes for our businesses. Just like in our adolescence, we often default to feelings rather than facts. We listen to our hearts instead of our heads. And we listen to our non-customers (family/friends) rather than our paying customers. We then find we're blocking our own success without even knowing it. We don't readily listen to those we don't yet trust – even if they may be trying to help us by pointing out our mindset blocks. Depending on the stage of our business career, we may feel we don't need to listen to them or change anything, as we're already enjoying a certain amount of success. However, at some point, we hit a mindset block (or more than one). We all do, including us as your authors. Then our business success becomes a self-fulfilling prophecy of "we can't" rather than "we can."

One pretty much sure-fire way of finding a mindset block is to suggest to a private healthcare professional that they should double their fees. Immediately, there will be excuse after excuse, generated by fear and insecurity, as to why they can't do this. Or there will be silent nods as they choose to ignore the suggestion. Occasionally, someone will step away from blocking their own success and enquire about the processes required to make such a bold move.

THE PROCESS OF RELEASE

The very first stage of overcoming an obstacle involves recognition that it needs to be overcome. We must recognise, and then accept, that a change is needed. As this floor is about releasing you from blocking your own progress, we'll focus on changing *you*. How often do you hear, *"I don't want to change"* or *"I can't change"*? That's usually proceeded by either *"I need to change"* or *"I don't need to change."* When improving your business, recognising the need to change is vital; without it, progress stalls, and potential evaporates. So how do you create recognition that change isn't only welcome – but necessary?

Unfortunately, lightbulb moments are different for each of us, as our various wants and needs fluctuate throughout our lives. Hearing, "You need to change," may not actually switch on any lightbulb for you. We normally need an internal driver to create our motivation to change. And that driver is usually (but not always) a pain point. Either we're currently in pain (not normally physical pain, but any mental anguish can manifest itself as such), or we're anticipating pain coming our way. This pain could present on an individual level and/or in the business itself:

INDVIDUAL	BUSINESS
Feeling sad	Poor cashflow
Problems concentrating	Reduced patient satisfaction
Insomnia	Increased complaints
Excessive use of drugs/ medication/alcohol	Time management problems
Inability to cope with stress	Reacting to "competitors"
Anger management issues	No updating of systems
Extreme changes in moods	No new equipment and/or services
Poor diet	Less staff engagement
Feeling not worthy / "imposter syndrome"	Rotting instead of growing

Sometimes pain comes not from our situation, but from a group to which we're connected – or in which we're invested emotionally or financially in some way. That pain could be due to sadness, anxiety, jealousy, anger, shame, or guilt. Humans don't tend to like pain, so we do what we can to avoid it. If we imagine pain as a wall in front of us, with a pain-free zone (our goal) on the other side of the wall, most of us would choose to walk around the wall to get to the other side. Some of us would go over the wall, depending upon its height. Fewer would choose to go through the wall, knocking it down in the process. The difficulty of this latter option, and the tools available to enable it, also correlates to how many choose this option. However, each of these options has its pros and cons:

GO ROUND	GO OVER	GO THROUGH
Easiest solution	Harder solution	Appears as hardest solution
Lowest energy/effort required	More energy/effort required	Most energy/effort required
Lowest satisfaction achieved	More satisfaction achieved	Most satisfaction achieved
Takes you furthest away from your goal	Higher risk of injury	Could be easiest solution with right tools to assist
Requires multiple changes in direction to reach your goal	Keeps you more on target for your goal	Requires learning how to do it safely, otherwise you'll feel vulnerable and open to more pain

You risk never reaching your goal, as you may get lost or sidetracked	You could lose sight of your goal but also could see beyond it	Once learnt, you have a new skill to help you in future
The wall will still exist and could block you again	The wall will still exist and could block you again	The wall would no longer exist (unless rebuilt), so it couldn't block you again

Going through and dealing with pain, rather than circumnavigating it, brings many benefits. These can include gaining skills that you didn't have before, satisfaction in doing something challenging, and developing a strategy for tackling future obstacles. The bigger and/ or stronger the wall of pain that you overcome, the more beneficial the outcomes can be for you. There will be short-term, hard work required, but how much and how difficult it is depends on what tools (if any) you enlist to help.

TOOLS TO ASSIST

Since you're reading this as a healthcare professional (or someone interested in the field), you're probably aware that our scientific understanding of pain has changed significantly in the past decade or so. We now realise pain is 100 percent an output from the brain, but there are ways our bodies fool us into believing it's located elsewhere. We think we experience physical pain far away from our brains, and we use treatments directed at that physical pain to alleviate it.

What if we could trick our brains into reducing our pain, so that we didn't experience it in our bodies? Well this is entirely possible, through working on our well-being. There are five key ways to improve our well-being, all of which will benefit our mental health and reduce the pain produced from our brains:

1. **Connect** – talk and listen to others, making connections with them and feeling like you're really there.
2. **Be Active** – keep your mind and body active through activities you enjoy, so that you can keep healthy and change your mood if needed.
3. **Take Notice** – be mindful and recall the simple things that bring you joy.
4. **Keep Learning** – embrace new experiences as they arrive, seek out new opportunities, and surprise yourself with what you can learn/do.
5. **Give** – offer yourself to others, as it will fulfil both you and them

By doing all these things, your capacity for pain will increase. But interestingly, you won't notice pain as much, because you'll feel happy, fulfilled, valued, and appreciated by others. These are the positive emotions you feel during growth. The more you help your well-being, the more resilience you build to help with any future pain that you may face. Whereas if you allow pain to overwhelm you, you'll get stuck – or even worse, go backwards, moving further away from your goal(s). Hence a need to change to overcome your pain points and achieve your dreams.

One of the most common pain points seen in many businesses – and healthcare ones are no exception – is with regards to "competitors." It seems counterintuitive to help them in any way, as potentially they could take patients away from you. But in reality, helping others to grow and other businesses to grow will actually help you and your business to grow. You may not realise this at the time of your providing that help, but further down the line, you'll reap the rewards.

So, the pain of having a business compete against you is best overcome by going through that pain – using the tools of support, help, engagement, and learning. All of those will benefit your business in the long term.

READY TO CHANGE

Once you've accepted the need to change, the first thing you must do is to let go of something. You do this to make room for something new, and hopefully better, to replace it.

Again, this can be done physically, in order that it benefits you mentally. Removing physical objects that constrain you can help release your brain to function better. Decluttering your life is a therapeutic process to release you from blocking your own success. By getting rid of physical things that you no longer need (such as items you haven't used or taken notice of for over a year), you gain a process that works for you. Over time, you can also use this learned method to shed the adopted behaviours that you no longer need. These behaviours exist due to your beliefs (and those of people around you), or as protective mechanisms against potential damage (from unwanted anxiety or hurt). But you don't need them in your present or future life.

Follow these eight steps for decluttering anything you no longer need:

1. **Start somewhere** – pick a shelf or cupboard you haven't accessed for quite some time, especially one with the least emotional stuff on or in it.
2. **Be optimistic** – think that you will aim to clear a set (high) percentage of items from the area you've picked.
3. **Be definite** – clear stuff to different piles, such as a disposal pile or donation pile (to someone else or a charity shop). Anything left can be returned to the area you're trying to clear.
4. **Record memories** – take photos of anything you feel emotionally connected to that you're worried you may forget without the physical memento, then donate or dispose of the item.
5. **Let it go** – there will be plenty of moments in your life when you don't want to let go of something, but the pain of that loss will subside in the weeks, months, or years to come.

6. **Enjoy the process** – decluttering can be cathartic, generating enjoyable relief and release from the past.
7. **Take a break** – if your mental energy starts to wane during the process, then stop for a (short) while. This will allow you to return with renewed energy and motivation to succeed in the task at hand.
8. **Get rid of items ASAP** – the sooner your piles make it to their destinations, the better it is for you. That way, there will be no time for changing your mind. Deleting old files and photos from your phone/tablet/computer/cloud storage can be fulfilling too. To help declutter mentally, consider writing down thoughts that are holding you back, and then disposing of that piece of paper in some way that is final, such as setting fire to it. All these methods will give you a sense of creating more space for new (better) thoughts and information, rather than just piling them on top of old thoughts and outdated information. You can also write down thoughts you want to build upon and seek reinforcement for; keeping a journal of these is worthwhile.

Sometimes you may struggle to give yourself permission to throw things away (physical or mental), so having support from someone who has gone through the same process can be beneficial. However, be wary of absolving yourself of responsibility or blaming someone else for any decisions made. This is your journey – wherein you're implementing your process and goals. The actions you take aren't theirs, and you'll only grow if you fully own your steps. Their input can also be useful for affirmations and evidence to support the positive thoughts you're keeping (and have written down!).

ACKNOWLEDGE GRIEF/LOSS/LETTING GO

Whenever we lose something from our lives, we experience some, if not all, of the stages of grief. Even if we engage in a change we welcomed, we inevitably feel some loss over what we let go of. Keeping a focus on the future and our vision for it will certainly help, but we cannot avoid grief.

There are five recognized stages of loss/grief (or seven, depending on the classification system used): denial, anger, bargaining, depression, acceptance. The severity and duration of each grief stage correlates to the significance to us of the thing we have lost – whether an object, person, or emotion. These stages often come in high waves initially, but they lessen over time. When decluttering or afterwards, if you experience any such waves, don't castigate yourself. Instead, just acknowledge the emotion, knowing that in due time, it won't feel so raw. It's important not to stall in your decluttering if you want to make progress. Keep clearing out the old to make room for the new.

BUILD YOUR DREAM AND FOCUS ON IT

To help you to let go of things that are holding you back, it's useful to have a vision of what is ahead of you. Focus on your dream of your better tomorrow, whatever that looks like for you (see Floor 1). The more you can define that dream, the clearer the image in your head, the more tangible it will be, and the more motivated you'll be to achieve it. By putting ever0-increasing detail into that dream, you'll find decluttering becomes easier, because you'll be able to ask yourself the simple question:

Does this feature in my future dream?

If it doesn't, then let it go, as it will not serve you on your journey or at your destination. This can include physical items or mental things (mindset blocks). You don't need them cluttering your vision, taking up space, and holding you back.

Make your dream multi-coloured with whistles and bells on it. Visualise it, draw it, describe it. Then share it with others who will support and encourage you. Once you've told people about your vision for your new future (no matter how much or little difference there is from your present), then you're more likely to reach your destination and achieve your dream.

Every day, you'll face distractions; it's just a fact of life. There will be demands on your time and energy that you may or may not have predicted, and these may prevent you from blocking your own progress. So, you must set some boundaries to help keep yourself focused on the job at hand. Schedule your day to maximise your efficiency and effectiveness. Plot the route to the future, allowing for contingencies, and set manageable targets. Regularly and repeatedly do something to take you further along that route. The more you do, the closer you'll get to your target. Focus clearly on the destination, looking forward to the future, rather than backwards to the past.

Remember that you can't change what has already happened, but you can change what is to come. If it helps, find yourself a mantra that you can repeat to keep you on track. Mantras can be used any time they may seem needed or helpful, but also during meditation sessions, which are useful for processing thoughts on any particular subject. There are plenty of mantras to choose from, and they really can help. Choose the one that resonates with you, and don't be afraid to change your mantra as you progress. Here are some options:

- Be in love with your life, every minute of it.
- Be a warrior, not a worrier.
- The difference between who you are and who you want to be is what you do.
- Positive mind, positive life.
- Feelings are not facts.
- Yesterday is not today.
- Inhale the future, exhale the past.
- I challenge myself because I'm fierce and stronger every day.
- I'm living an empowered life.
- I was born to be real, not to be perfect.

- Anxiety is contagious, and so is calm.
- Be brave, take risks; nothing can substitute experience.
- I'm determined and disciplined; when I set my mind to something, anything is possible.
- The best way to get something done is to begin.
- The sun always rises, and the sun always sets.
- Success is not rocket science.
- Be the best version of yourself.

IGNORE THE NEGATIVE VOICES

We all have them – those voices mentioned at the beginning of this floor. Our ability to silence them, ignore them, or overcome them is what will reflect on our ability to be successful, transform, and grow. Ignoring the negative voices isn't always easy to do, but the more practised you become, the simpler it gets. The quickest route is to stop listening to the negative external voices. Other people will be quick to judge you and the decisions you make, especially if your decisions conflict with their worldviews. The sooner you stop listening to others, with their own mindset blocks, the sooner you'll let go of your own.

And it's quite easy to do! Just surround yourself with a tribe of those who will support your transformation and have developed their own skills in letting go. These are the trailblazers who have broken the mould, and those who will likewise support you in the process. Similarly, let go of those around you who won't be part of your future. You'll know the ones; they don't bring you any real joy or fulfilment. They drain you more than encourage you. They wait for you to make an effort, rather than making an effort themselves. They'd rather reiterate and reinforce their own mindset blocks than talk about how you're overcoming yours.

These people will just hold you back. They won't be loyal for the duration of your journey, especially after they've finished using you.

And use you they will, before effectively stabbing you in the back with their words of criticism and condemnation. Don't let your relationships be a one-way street. Take control and move away from their negative influences. In so doing, you'll make room for more positive ones. Finding new friends, relationships, and challenges helps with the process of letting go of others. It takes you out of your comfort zone, which is good for your growth, and it fulfils the requirements for your well-being.

Once you've put distance between yourself and the external, negative voices – and surrounded yourself with new, more positive ones – you'll find it much easier to diminish your internal, negative voice. This is the one that makes you second-guess everything you do. It creates an imposter syndrome, which holds you back from achieving all that you're capable of. Acknowledge that this voice exists, but realise that it's a throwback to your past (frequently your childhood). If necessary, give that voice what it needs to appease it – recognition and reassurance – but don't dwell on its negative words. Move forward – using one of your mantras if it helps – and leave the voice happily chasing its tail in a small corner of your brain. Know that it will return, but the more skilled you become at dealing with it, the less impact it will have on you. With practice, it will become even easier to release yourself from your mindset blocks.

EXERCISE
Facts and Beliefs

One way to appease your negative inner voice is to logically process it. This involves looking at *what are the facts* and *what are the beliefs* in any given situation or change requirement. Here are some steps to follow:

STEP1: Grab a pen and paper.

STEP 2: Write statements of several factors that seem to be blocking you from achieving success or your vision (see Floor 1), such as:
- *"My patients can't afford it."*
- *"I can't speak in public or record a video."*
- *"There's no parking at my clinic."*
- *"It's too difficult to change."*

STEP 3: Take each statement and consider in depth whether it's a *fact* or just your *belief* about a situation.

STEP 4: Record your answer next to each one.

You may struggle at times to decide if something is a fact or a belief. You may end up hitting a *belief barrier*, which occurs when you can't overcome a restrictive block. Breaking the belief down into smaller parts to more easily overcome the barrier is one method you could use.

Remember when you first learnt to drive or swim? You probably thought that it was really difficult. You may even have doubted your ability. So you had lessons – and lots of them, so you could build on prior learning each time. This continued after you passed any tests, until it became second nature to just drive or swim. Now apply that concept to a belief you hold regarding your business. One of the most common ones is that "patients won't pay more." Well, that can be broken down into which patients (demographics, hobbies/interests, their presenting pathologies, etc.) will or won't, what action they will or won't they take, and how much or how little is "more"? By addressing each of these separately, you'll see that your *belief barrier* isn't insurmountable in all cases. In fact, it may be far more readily overcome than you first thought.

You may want to enlist the help of others. By going through the process of assessing facts versus beliefs in a small group, the beliefs will soon show themselves. Some in the group won't share your beliefs, whereas the facts should be the same for everyone. Once you've separated the facts from the beliefs, you can then look at what's required to change those beliefs if needed, often by making use of the facts you've identified.

This is a powerful tool that will help you to let go, and it can be used in so many other situations. If we take the "patients won't pay more" example, and you later found that certain types of patients would pay a lot more without any negative effect, then that fact would help overcome your original belief.

Dear Jill – Do You Beat Yourself Up, and If So, How Do You Stop It?

Sometimes, no matter how much positive thinking or mindfulness we practice, life just gets busy, balls get dropped, and we beat ourselves up over it.

A while ago, I went through a major spell of self-beating when my husband and I moved back to the UK from Turkey. Now I know widely-touted stats that state moving house is the second most stressful thing you'll deal with in your life (after the death of a loved one, we believe). But my husband and I are pretty expert at it; this was our tenth move in twelve years. There are a lot of moving parts in these situations, yes, and life does get a bit more frenetic for a while, but we find that's generally as tough as it gets.

We all have these things that crop up in our lives and complicate matters, and running our own business just adds to the melee at times like that. There's a lot to deal with, and it isn't always sensible to try and do it all at once.

The week before we moved out of our house, I launched my new free training programme that would lead seamlessly into my new, virtual, live, marketing training programme. Yay!!!

The plan was simple: get it up and running with all the tech in place to put it on autopilot, and gain four weeks to focus on moving and having some down time. In our plans, there were farewell drinks, goodbye lunches, a few days away with a girlfriend, time relaxing in our luxury hotel, flying home, a week's holiday with family, moving into our temporary accommodation (while our furniture made the journey), a week's holiday with friends. Then, finally, we'd get to moving in and turning our new house into our home, with new neighbours to meet and a new neighbourhood to explore.

All the while, I was going to develop my new website and be ready to launch my first live training programme in September – plus write twelve articles for a monthly column I'd promised a publisher. Simple.

Simple, at least until two days before we moved out of our house – when the tech went pear-shaped and began to unravel. My slick automation died, the slightly frustrated recipients were (rightly) complaining, our hotel Wi-Fi created a conflict with my website software, our temporary accommodation had no Wi-Fi, we felt guilty about spending holiday time with family and friends while focussed on work, and my husband (quite rightly) wanted me to help find our new car and get the house straight as quickly as possible when we moved in. I tried to do it all simultaneously!

The voices inside of my head were SHOUTING at me: write the articles, your website isn't going to develop itself, get that bug fixed, there are e-mails to respond to, the course won't ever be ready to launch – You're Rubbish!! And you're so going to get rumbled for being soooooo rubbish!!!!

I was trying to balance completing my planned work and panic-broken website – while relaxing, seeing friends and family, and having a holiday – alongside packing, moving, and unpacking. Guess what? It didn't work. I couldn't engage 100 percent with any of it, so we missed precious moments, I lost sleep, and we felt bad about it!! Really bad! I had an internal battle between doing what needed to be done for my business, to get moved, or to enrich my life.

Fast forwarding four weeks – having moved into our new house and surrounded by chaos (but still with no internet) – I agreed to go with some new neighbours to the horse races for Ladies' Day. I also agreed that over the weekend, my husband and I would have our first soirée into town, as well as start work on taming the garden, making curtains, putting up shelves, painting old furniture, hanging pictures, putting furniture in place...the list went on.

An afternoon at the races was a lovely thought, but I was internally stressing about the wasted time I could be using on the website or doing some writing. All the while, I knew we needed down time, and we needed to get the house set up so we could get on with our lives. There were so many voices shouting in my head that I thought it would explode!

On Friday morning, I tried to work on the website – in between holding things while my husband measured and drilled, and sewing some curtains. By the time we got ourselves all dressed up and on the minibus at lunch time, I felt stressed and not in the mood for fun.

The voices were there again: you could be...you should be...you must be...! As we drove through the city, watching new streets and sites go by and listening to my fellow passengers laughing and joking, I realised that if I didn't turn the voices off, I'd have a truly miserable time, and my internal struggle would carry on for much longer. So there and then, I decided to silence the voices and have a brilliant weekend.

That was it. Decision made. I, Jill Woods, would have fun, and to heck with it. I gave myself permission to have some down time. Making that conscious decision to turn the voices off worked brilliantly. It was raining and very overcast at the races, but I had a great time: watching the horses and people, getting to know new friends, eating delicious fish and chips, watching the races, and having a few little bets. It was brilliant fun, and I was relaxed for the first time in what felt like months. The day was capped off with nine of us around our hastily-erected dining table, eating a Chinese takeaway and chatting like old friends.

The rest of the weekend was spent in shorts and T-shirts – enjoying the sunshine whilst gardening, painting, sewing, building furniture, and setting up home. We went out for coffee, brunch, and lunch. It was brilliant. I didn't think about or look at my website or work once.

This was all possible to achieve because I could silence the voices in my head by giving myself permission to ignore the things that were dragging me down – i.e., work. So come Monday morning, I sat at my desk with renewed focus, having experienced a wonderful and rewarding weekend. As a result, our home was all sorted, my website was fixed, the articles got written, more people than ever signed up to my free programme, and I had some quality downtime without the accompanying negative voices. Wonderful!

HAVE FUN

They say that laughter is the best medicine, but it can also help to release us. By having fun, we soon forget the negative emotions and implications of any change we're facing. It reminds us that life is for living, that good times can be had in the face of adversity, and that the simplest things can bring us happiness.

So, make time in your busy life to have some fun. The activities vary from person to person, but whatever you consider fun, be absorbed by it for a period of time. Live in that moment, love the feelings it brings, and experience its regenerative and rejuvenating properties.

In our opinion, watching mindless TV or YouTube videos doesn't count as a fun activity that releases or enriches you in the ways we're describing. If you don't believe that you have time for fun in your life (and it's only a belief, not a fact!), then ditch the watching – unless it's related to learning – and engage with something that fulfils your soul.

You'll be amazed at how much more you can achieve, how much more fun you can have, and how many more memories you can create from experiences and personal interactions. The latter will give you such support as you grow, which will be much-needed to reassure you that you may bend, but you won't break – especially if those with whom you engage fully support and encourage your journey.

Find your tribe of those who will 100 percent back you, as you let go of the blocks stopping your own progress.

ACTION POINTS TO ENSURE YOU HAVE LET GO

☐ Connect with others

☐ Decide to be active

☐ Make sure you take notice

☐ Commit to keep on learning

☐ Give yourself to others

☐ Declutter your life

☐ Focus on your dream

☐ Ignore the negative voices

☐ Complete the Facts & Beliefs exercise

☐ Have fun

YOU'VE NOW LET GO √

NOTES

FLOOR 3 – ENGAGE:

Building Your Successful Business
and a Happy You

- ✓ Intentionally build your practice.
- ✓ Don't attract all types of patients.
- ✓ Build a tribe of patients who love you.
- ✓ Build a patient referral network.
- ✓ Declutter your work environment.
- ✓ Understand your "why".

Once you've established your vision and started working on releasing the mental blocks preventing you from achieving that vision, you can move forward to focus on your healthcare practice. This floor is all about intentionally creating a business that serves both you and your patients, making you very happy in the process.

Too many health practitioners are running their businesses on autopilot. They go through the motions every day to keep their practice running, but without any clear goal or path to the practice of their dreams.

Creating that *dream practice* is totally doable. Just look around you, and I'm sure you'll find healthcare practices (not necessarily in your area of clinical practice) that look and feel like the kind of business you'd love to own. But to end up with the business you want, which also serves both you and your patients, you must get intentional and engaged. Each decision you make and action you take must move you towards the business that you desire.

Every decision you make about your business should come from a place of desire and dreaming — and be something that contributes to your happiness.

For some, the idea of being happy at work can feel decadent or selfish. But in reality, it's essential. Doing so helps you feel aligned with your business – achieving a state of happiness at work so that you bring the best version of yourself to your patients and team every day. Getting engaged and focused is an act of kindness, not an act of selfishness.

Yes, of course there will be tough days when things don't go quite as you want. But as you get more engaged with this business-building process and focused on making decisions that intentionally move you in a specific direction, your days will feel more aligned with who you are and the dreams you have. When that process becomes the norm, you'll be more onboard with your decisions. Then, working through the tough tasks or days becomes easier.

Consequently, the opposite is true. You'll be less engaged with decisions that aren't aligned to you and your business vision, or which don't inspire happiness. You'll be less fulfilled by these activities, and therefore less likely to see them to completion. Procrastination is a great indicator that you're not engaged in working towards something that really excites you.

Building a successful healthcare business also means building a happy healthcare professional. We're not talking instant gratification here, like a patient bringing in a cream cake or a bottle of wine for you (although that can make you smile). We're talking about happiness that's fulfilling – engaging you in living and loving your life, making your work an absolute pleasure, helping you cope when things don't go so well and challenges arise.

All too often, we hear from practitioners who aren't happy in their practices. They moan about their patients, they have no free time, they're frustrated about money, and even worse, they're thinking of leaving their business – either leaving their chosen healthcare profession completely or dreaming of early retirement. They're deeply unhappy at work and in their businesses.

Has this happened to you? Usually, this happens when you've lost your way – when your practice, patients, or team members are calling the shots. Often you're taking in every single patient that crosses your path, whether they're the right patients for you or not. They may or may not present with something you enjoy treating, something you're good at treating, or something you have all the facilities and skills to treat. Also, people get disillusioned while working ridiculously long hours, to the detriment of their personal lives, without being rewarded financially or emotionally for their sacrifices.

These kinds of practices often come about by accident, when the lead practitioner or owner doesn't hold a clear vision for the business, hasn't set in place clear boundaries, and isn't actively engaged every day with intentionally building the desired practice. The direction of (and engagement in) your practice isn't something you want to be passive about or leave to chance. If you're not actively engaged with choosing exactly what your business is, how and where it operates, who it works with, what it sells, and why you're operating in the first place, then you're more than likely working really hard at creating an accidental business and not a practice by design.

Too many practices we see aren't the result of the hopes, dreams, and vision of a great practitioner. They're instead a conglomeration of random events, ideas, and circumstances – all of which result in a practice that's neither serving the patients or the team members to its best, nor is it likely bringing those practitioners happiness and fulfilment.

To create a practice that really makes you happy, you must get really clear on what must happen. Your happiness in your practice is largely based on six clear elements:

1. **Who** you work with – the patients and team members around you.
2. **Where** you work – the environment you're immersed in every day.
3. **What** you sell – the treatments and products you offer.
4. **When** you work – the hours and days you treat patients and run your business.
5. **Why** you run the practice – the purpose behind your daily investment of time and energy.
6. **How** you work – the processes and systems that dictate how you engage in your practice.

The decisions you make around each of these six elements is what will dictate your satisfaction and happiness in private practice. Let's explore each factor and get honest about how intentionally you're building each element – rather than leaving these things to chance.

WHO YOU WORK WITH?

Let's start by focusing on *who* you work with. Hopefully it goes without saying that those who surround you will greatly impact how you feel at the end of each day. Many people engage with the day-to-day functioning of any healthcare practice – including the owner, team members (clinical and support staff), patients, local referrers, suppliers, other local businesses, and the wider local community.

To be successful and run a thriving, happy practice, you must nurture relationships with specific kinds of people in each of the following categories. Some categories will impact your happiness more than others. Let's go through them one by one and explore how you can become more intentional about surrounding yourself with the right people.

YOUR TEAM

Let's start by reviewing the people in your immediate environment: your team. You need people on your team who share the same values and vision, but who also bring more to the party. You all must be pulling in the same direction, representing a unified front. Patients need to feel they're in safe hands with a team that has their very best interests at heart.

However, team members who challenge you by putting new ideas on the table are a great asset to any practice. You won't grow as a person or practice if everyone is just like you. Successful teams are made up of people pulling in the same direction, while bringing different skills and strengths to the party.

While recruiting, consider which professional qualifications are essential for professional registration, etc. Then recruit based on personality, values, and ethics. Skills can be taught – even if it takes time. Personality, vision, and values often aren't even considered at recruitment – yet successful practices will pay close attention to these factors, knowing how crucial they are.

If someone isn't naturally aligned with the values and ethos of the practice, they won't fit in, help the future of the practice, or stay very long.

If the absolute right person shows up but doesn't have some of the technical skills or knowledge you'd like, they're still the right person to employ. They'll naturally fit in, be aligned to how you work, and over time can learn what you need them to do. You can further cement their place in your team by offering the opportunity for continuing professional development or mentoring to improve any skills you feel need attention. In doing so, you upskill your workforce and engender great loyalty for investing and showing trust in them.

As the team leader, you have a vital role in clearly communicating your vision for the practice, any professional boundaries, the values by which you work, your expectations of your team's delivery, and your desired systems and processes. Nine times out of ten, if someone isn't performing in their role, it's not their fault, it's yours. You either put someone in a role they weren't equipped for, or you failed to provide detailed instructions and support to help them carry out their role. Failure to educate, train, communicate, and support lies squarely at your door, not theirs. Even if your team is just you and a part-time receptionist or locum practitioner, their training and development is still your responsibility.

Building a cohesive and aligned team from the ground up will give your patients that warm and fuzzy feeling about your practice, as well as give you the competitive edge and a successful business. Too many employees in small businesses are employed to fill a specific role, rather than allowed to incorporate their natural talents and skills. Yet these special abilities could really help develop the practice. Giving team members a degree of ownership in the practice by including them – and their skills and interests – in the development process will build loyalty, provide career progression, and reap great rewards for everyone.

YOUR PATIENTS

The other group of people who surround you every day are your patients. Having the right patients in your practice is just as important as having the right team members. Every practice needs a bunch of raving fans – a.k.a. happy patients. They will become raving fans if they're the right patients for you from the outset.

These people must love what you do, love how you do it, and most importantly love *you*! Apathetic patients fill appointments in your diary, but they don't bring that positive energy, fun, and enthusiasm that engages your team and enlivens your environment. Your tribe of raving fans also become the best marketing team you could ever wish for.

It may feel counterintuitive not to pursue every patient that contacts your practice, but having disengaged patients who aren't aligned with your strengths or values can negatively impact your practice. You'll waste time trying to make them happy, and they may leave poor reviews, etc. They also can take twice as much time to serve – costing you money and authority in the long run.

Knowing who you want to fill your appointments with is essential, so you can attract more of them. You basically need a tribe of patients who love you, and most likely these will be the patients you love to see. To help grow your fan base, we'll share more detail on Floor 5. But for now, just be aware that the patients in your practice are impacting your happiness.

Dear Jonathan – How Have Your Patients Changed Over the Years to Enable You to Be Happier?

> *When I first opened my private podiatry practice, I thought I had to be all things "feet" to all people. So I filled my clinic with anyone and everyone who would pay my*

low fees at the time. I soon filled up my clinic and spent my days going from highs to lows, satisfaction to discontent, and fulfilment to frustration. This kept happening, week in and week out. I just couldn't understand why.

Then one of my patients who was experienced in business gave me a nugget of wisdom: Increase your prices if you're too busy. You'll earn as much without seeing as many patients.

So I did, and guess what happened? I lost some patients! But the patients I lost weren't the ones I was fussed about losing. They were the ones who seemed to contribute to the lows, discontent, and frustration of my work. They were the ones who moaned about small fee increases, or weren't interested in any new knowledge/ equipment I'd invested in, or didn't follow the advice I gave them to improve their health.

As I started to assess my patients further, I realised there were four types, and my happiness was suffering because I was attracting too many of the types I didn't want. The types are:

1. ***Awesome Patients*** *– these patients love you and sing your praises to anyone and everyone (including leaving online reviews). For me, these include patients willing to invest their time and money in their foot health.*
2. ***Benign Patients*** *– these patients do you no harm; they like you and are happy to recommend you if asked, but they aren't as proactive as A patients.*
3. ***Cost-Conscious Patients*** *– these patients question any price changes or don't see the value of looking after their feet properly. They devalue your sense of worth.*
4. ***Dire Patients*** *– these patients complain at the slightest thing, using bullying tactics that create a negative emotional response from you, which affects the rest of your day.*

Once I understood these types – and that I couldn't please all the people all the time – I actively discouraged types 3 and 4 from coming to my clinic. As a result, my day became filled with type 1 and 2 patients. These brought happiness and positivity to my workday, and I reciprocated the same to them. Today, my work-life is good!

LOCAL REFERRERS

Next let's look at your local referrers. How many other local businesses or healthcare professionals refer new patients directly to your practice? Proactively engaging with building a network of these local referrers can reap huge rewards for your practice. It's a great way to create a steady flow of quality new patients (type 1 and 2 – the ones you want in your practice). But not many practices strategically do this so that resulting relationships become long-lasting, mutually beneficial, and professional.

To create a Patient Referral Network, you must develop a small, cohesive network (not a random list) of other local people who already have the eyes and ears of large numbers of your potential dream patients. But these people also must be ones whose dream clients, members, or patients may be your existing patients. These could be:

- Other healthcare professionals
- Sports coaches
- Self-care business owners like beauticians or hairdressers
- Personal trainers
- Therapists
- Social group managers
- Community club organisers
- Nursing home or care facility managers

This is important for a number of reasons, but primarily because it gives you access to other professionals to refer to. These are people who will treat your patients well and make you look professional and well-connected. And they can also serve as a potential source of new patients for you.

Once you identify the key contacts in your network, work hard at investing time, energy, money, and attention into nurturing these relationships. If you support them in their business and organisations, they'll likely support you in yours. You can support each other with:

- **Cross referrals** – providing them with mutual referrals to new clients.
- **Educational support** – helping to train or educate their team members about what a podiatrist or chiropractor really does.
- **Practical support** – sharing business know-how and experience.
- **Emotional support** – helping them through a rough patch or celebrating when their business takes off.

Note that this all takes time and energy. Therefore, choose the people you'd like to include in your network wisely, and keep the number small. That said, these are people who could potentially have a big impact in your life and in your business, so it's worth the investment to build these strong relationships.

A little note about the people…...First, the people you want in your Patient Referral Network must be those who feel in some way aligned to you, either professionally, personally, emotionally, or through their values and ethics. You don't need them to be your new best friends, but there must be some connection for an authentic, long-lasting relationship to work.

Second, you must share mutual professional respect. If they don't particularly respect your work of say, being a podiatrist or an orthopaedic surgeon, then that relationship won't work. You must mutually and confidently be able to cross-refer patients, knowing they will be well looked after. You'll also want to align with those who you genuinely want in your business or organisation.

If you can save your patient from needing to hunt around for a solution to a problem that you can't directly solve, and your referral turns out to be a great help, the patient will think you're both heroes.

Consider those in your Patient Referral Network as people you want to develop a long and successful relationship with. Don't fall into the trap of just viewing them as your new patient conveyor belt, delivering patients to you on a one-way track. Prepare to invest in nurturing these relationships. Reciprocate any energy or referrals sent your way.

Managing Expectations

Each party within the Patient Referral Network also needs to understand what the other wants or expects. This includes the quality of the people you cross refer, as well as the service and care that will be provided. Engage in a conversation about expectations, so you can both be confident and happy in making those referrals. Otherwise, the process may become a very one-sided, which isn't a recipe for a long-standing relationship.

Some relationships may be much less formal, while others may be more structured. You must be clear on things like the system of referral, appointment availability, exchange of information, and follow-up reporting after appointments (with patient consent), etc. Discuss the exact process, so both parties understand how it will work – and make sure you deliver that as a minimum service. When possible, try and do more or go that extra mile either for the patient or the referrer. Give each other total confidence to keep referring.

SUPPLIERS

Next, let's look at suppliers. These are people who impact your happiness to a lesser extent than your team and patients, but they still warrant some intentional engagement.

Doing business with organisations that feel like a good fit makes life in business a bit more pleasant. You'll want to work with those suppliers who do business well. You can recognize these individuals. because they work efficiently, deliver on time, communicate effectively, resolve issues quickly, and are generally nice people. These are the ones who generally make life in your practice happier.

Using suppliers who are aligned to your values and ethics feels good, too. Consider whether they: sell products you love and which work well, are concerned about sustainability, source products ethically, pay fair wages, or support charities you care about. All of these factors can contribute to how you feel about working with a certain supplier. Where suppliers of products or services are limited, you may not have a choice. But where there's a choice, get picky.

OTHER LOCAL BUSINESSES

Next, think about your local business community. We've talked already about those businesses that are potential mass referrers, but there will also be a community of other local businesses who, just by the fact they're local to you, can support your business journey.

They may not be mass referrers, but they may refer the odd person to you – or they could also be great business friends. It doesn't matter how big or small your local business community is, you can still reach out and build friendships and a network of business buddies who will support you through tough times with a smile, a hug, and a drink on a Friday night. They might support you by helping connect you to the best accountant or marketing copywriter in town. They might support you by cross promoting an event you're running or providing prizes for a charity event you're holding. Your local business friends can support you in a myriad of ways, which really can make the difference when it comes to happiness in your practice. Think about ways of engaging and nurturing relationships with these local business owners.

YOUR WIDER COMMUNITY

Now that we've looked at local businesses, next think about local clubs/organisations that you could connect with, build relationships with, and support with your expertise, time, and energy. This can really add to the quality of life you experience.

Consider collaborating with organisations like sports, social, or community clubs – whose staff or members you could support with health promotion talks or equipment demonstrations a few times a year. Or talk to your local school, whose teachers you could support by providing a lesson once a year on an element of biology and the national curriculum, or a careers talk.

Consider supporting local charities which you feel aligned with, where you could run events within or donate your products or services. Getting involved with a local charity is a great way to pay it forward as well as raise your profile and help more people.

The list goes on, but we're sure you get the picture. The more varied people you can actively engage with and involve in your business, the more your business will thrive and spark your joy. Think about a rock concert or sporting event in a large stadium. With only a few apathetic spectators present, the event would feel lackluster. Put just a few excited people in the stadium, and the atmosphere can start to change. Enthusiasm and excitement are contagious. At the next event, there will be more excited people. As the positive energy grows and the word spreads, more people will want to get tickets and be part of what's happening. This is the feeling you want to engender in and around your practice. Feeling supported, encouraged, and championed by other people in your local area will boost your confidence and shape how you feel about your practice.

At the end of the day, who you work and surround yourself with is entirely your choice. Get engaged with choosing, not just accepting what is.

WHERE YOU WORK

The environment you spend so much time in every day can greatly impact how you feel. Yet so many practices – conditioned by what they see within their industry, and their personal experience of being a patient in other kinds of medical practices – replicate bland, cookie-cutter, non-remarkable environments.

We've all been there. You approach the building, and there's nothing remarkable about the exterior. There's a smartly-painted front door with a brass plaque off to the right – or maybe a vinyl transfer on a glass window, showing the logo of the practice. You walk in, and there's a faint whiff of clinical cleaner or other chemical-based products. The first sight to greet you is a tall reception desk that's obliterating your view of the receptionist behind it.

You look around, and even though you've never been here before, it looks so familiar. There's a radio playing in the background and a tall-but-slightly-jaded Yucca plant over in the corner. A row or two of padded vinyl chairs line the walls of the waiting area. One or two notice boards appear covered in clearly-old posters and postcards extolling the virtues of various treatments available or highlighting where previous patients have been on holiday. There's an ever-so-polite notice laminated about twenty years ago, asking visitors not to eat in the waiting area. And on a low-level melamine table, there's a collection of dogeared magazines that were published anywhere between a month and three years ago. The walls not covered with notice boards are painted magnolia and display either certificates of accomplishments of the clinical team or slightly faded framed prints of the old masters.

In the corner, there's a brightly-coloured plastic crate containing children's toys discarded by the practice owners' children at least ten years before. And if you're lucky, in the other corner sits a water cooler where you can help yourself. If you take the time to look up, you'll see ceiling tiles, strip lights, and possibly spotlights on a track for lighting. If you venture into the treatment room – whether you're at the dentist, optician, chiropractor, podiatrist, physiotherapist, or naturopath – there's a really good chance that the same monotony will continue.

And let's not forget the other spaces in many practices: washroom facilities, assessment areas, team common rooms and/or kitchens, equipment preparation areas, practice offices, corridors, and staircases joining them all together. Collectively, this is the environment you work in every day.

How does yours measure up on the blandometer? How would it fair on the inspiringometer or wonderfulometer? *Unremarkable* isn't great from a marketing perspective, especially when you're trying to stand out from the crowd. But it's definitely not good for your morale when really you want to work in an environment that you love, feel inspired by, and take pride in.

CLUTTER

OK, let's talk about the elephant in the room: clutter. On Floor 2, we talked about how we must declutter our lives to help ourselves let go. But what about clutter in our work environment?

> Working in a cluttered environment isn't great for you. Clutter reduces your ability to focus, impacts your short-term memory, can make you more anxious, reduces your productivity, and decreases your ability to process information.

In short, working (and living, for that matter) in a cluttered environment isn't good for us. And as we have discussed, that which isn't good for us impacts the quality of the service we provide to our patients.

EXERCISE
Decluttering

Take yourself into your practice on a day when there's no one else there (this takes a few hours). Bring a notebook with a page headed "Things to Be Replaced," two cardboard boxes labelled "Get Rid Of" and "Move," and some sticky notes for items too big for the boxes. Simply walk round each room in the practice, touch every single thing in the room, and ask yourself:

1. *Does this (thing you're touching) have an essential role to play in making our practice brilliant?* – Yes or No? If no, put it in the Get Rid Of box. Or if it's too big for the box, attach a Get Rid Of sticky note. If yes, ask:
2. *Is it the best version of this thing we could have?* – Yes or No? If yes, leave it where it is, and move on to question 2. If no, add the item to the Things to Be Replaced page in your notebook, but remember to get rid of the original item once replaced.
3. *Is this the best location for it to do its job?* – Yes or No? If no, put it in the Move box, or attach a sticky note with Move on it. Don't stop and start moving things to their destination right away, as you'll break the flow of the task in hand. If yes, awesome! Leave it there. and transition to the next item.

After you finish in each room or area, move all the things that need moving, so you know that room is complete before you go onto the next room. Just keep moving around the practice a room at a time, touching everything and asking yourself these questions. Before long, we're pretty confident you'll have things in your Get Rid Of box and lots of items with sticky notes, as well as a list of things that you want to upgrade. We also suspect that by the end, you'll be looking for better storage solutions, while feeling much calmer and less over-whelmed by stuff.

Once you've done your decluttering, then you can move onto reviewing how your practice looks inside. So get your thinking cap on and start reviewing your current environment. The list of things you have control over in relation to aesthetics is actually huge when you stop to reflect. We want to ask you, consider if you're blissfully happy with your:

- Flooring
- Decorations
- Windows
- Smells
- Wall and ceiling colours
- Display stands
- Seating
- Storage facilities
- Door handles
- Soft furnishings
- Shelves
- Waste disposal facilities
- Dispensers
- Cupboard and drawer fronts
- Coat hooks
- Storage for wet umbrellas
- Door mats
- Occasional tables
- Refreshment facilities
- Reading material
- Pictures and frames
- Plants
- Door and drawer handles
- Window coverings
- Specialist equipment
- Plumbing fixtures

We could go on, but we're sure you get the idea. There are so many elements that combine to create the environment you work in every day. How engaged have you been with intentionally choosing elements that you (and your patients) will love?

Note about home visiting practices: If your practice delivers all or even some of its services in other people's spaces, your choices are limited on what you can do to make that space inspiring, welcoming, or more functional. But still, take time to be engaged with the process of intentionally making yourself happier with the environment. You can do simple things like:

- Driving there in a car you love
- Wearing clothes that make you feel confident, professional, and fabulous
- Only using the best mobile equipment you can afford (you may revisit your fees – see Floor 4)
- Only using equipment that works well for you in the mobile environment, like that which is light to carry or makes your working space more effective
- Having mobile payment facilities that enable simple and effective payments
- Having access to a digital diary, so rebooking appointments is easy and efficient.

How would you love your environment to function, look, and feel? It's your choice, but we'd urge you to get much more engaged with these specifics. If you need inspiration, just go to Pinterest and search for "clinical interiors." That will give you some food for thought (and potentially make three hours of your evening disappear!). At the end of the day, your work location is entirely your choice. Get engaged with choosing, not just accepting what is.

WHAT YOU SELL

The services you provide in your practice don't need to include every clinical skill you ever learnt in training. Similarly, the products that you sell don't need to include every product available in your area of clinical practice. Just because the practice down the road delivers specific services that fall within the scope of practice for your profession doesn't mean that you must.

What you deliver for your patients in terms of services and products is entirely up to you.

You get to choose services that:

- You're good at
- You enjoy delivering
- You get great results from
- Your dream patients really need
- Your dream patients really value
- You have the facilities to deliver really well.

You get to sell products that:

- You've seen work really well
- Are easy for your patients to use
- Deliver fast results
- Are made from high-quality components
- Fit with your ethics and values
- Carry a designer tag that your dream patients will love
- Are highly respected in your industry
- Provide your patients with great value for their money.

In relation to working with rather than competing with other local practices, you can develop a wonderful, symbiotic relationship. For example, as each of you could develop specialty areas of practice, you can refer patients across the road to the practice that specialises in the treatment you don't want to offer.

Also, putting together packages of services and physical products gives you really clear "products" of your own to sell. Over time, you can develop these packages, focusing on the services and physical products you love which also work well, are highly profitable, and your dream patients see real value in. You can focus these packages on practice areas that you want to become famous for locally. Over time, that's exactly what will happen.

You spend so much of your time hands-on with clients and patients that in order to be happy in your practice, you must be engaged with identifying those clinical treatments and physical products that you love the most. Then, build more and more of them into your working day. At the end of the day, the products and services you sell are entirely your choice. Get engaged with choosing, not just accepting what is.

WHEN YOU WORK

The hours and times that you work also contribute to how happy you will feel about your practice. Getting engaged with choosing the following will give you a sense of control, knowing that your practice isn't ruling your life.

Have you chosen:

- What days you work?
- What times each day you work?
- What hours each week you work?
- How many days a week you want to work?
- How much time off you take?
- If you work weekends?
- If you work public holidays?
- If you always take a lunch break?
- How you fit in emergencies?
- Whether you're happy to do admin work during evenings or weekends?

Getting really clear on these decisions, setting boundaries around the times you do and don't want to be working, and enforcing those boundaries, can positively impact how happy you're working in and on your practice.

In some instances, it can make really great business sense to offer appointments early in the morning, late at night, and seven days a week. But this is where your engagement really comes in. Just because a business practice might be right for the bottom line in your business doesn't always make it the right thing for you to do. You must get honest with what hours and when you really want to be working.

In the early days of our practices, I think most of us fall into the mode of "work as many hours as you can just to get the cashflow rolling," without really thinking through the personal implications. Often businesses need that extra work just to gain some initial momentum. But just accepting that as the status quo for the rest of your practice-owning life won't necessarily help you build a practice that makes you really happy.

None of your business habits need to be set in stone forever. You can change your mind about how an aspect of your business looks over time. Your patients will respond well to consistency, so don't chop and change too frequently. But also don't be afraid to regularly assess your working hours to ensure your decisions still support your desired quality of life.

If you're currently feeling less than inspired by your practice, your inclination when faced with these questions may be quite different than how you would reply while feeling inspired and excited by your work. If you're currently at a low ebb in one or all of the six areas we've discussed on this floor, you may decide you only want to work one day a week in the practice. Or, once you've reviewed your six happiness-bringing elements, you may feel much more excited and inspired and want to be in the practice five days a week. There's no golden rule other than to do what feels right for you. When you work is entirely your choice. Get engaged with choosing, not just accepting what is.

WHY YOU RUN THE PRACTICE

Why do you put yourself through all of this? What is your driver for investing the hours and emotional and physical energy every day to run your practice? Understanding why you're doing this can help you get a handle on setting boundaries, making strategic decisions, and aligning your business with your life vision.

Again, like all of these six elements, so many health practices are just sailing blindly in no particular direction, because they've never really engaged with understanding what their *why* is. Can you state really clearly why you're engaged in your practice? Your why – the reason you're putting all of this time, energy, and money into your practice – is often made up of three elements. It's often something that:

- Makes you happy
- Involves serving other people
- Is connected to an emotion

> Your why will guide you like a compass.
> It shines a light on where you're going.

Your why can provide real clarity around the direction needed to achieve what you say you want. It becomes the filter through which you can pass the business development decisions you make every day. Your why will change over time, because it has four levels of maturity. With time in business, you'll shift from one to another. Those four levels are:

1. **Survival** – in this phase, your why is usually connected to making enough money to pay the bills.
2. **Status** – in this phase, your why is often connected to attaining success (whatever that looks like for you).
3. **Freedom** – in this phase, your why can be driven by attaining enough money and time to do and have more of what you want.

4. **Purpose** – in this phase, your why is often connected to contributing. That could be financially, or through sharing your expertise or giving freely of your time.

Your why can offer a new way of viewing your business journey, providing real meaning behind your actions. Rather than just working every day to pay the bills, which can feel very soulless or without purpose, understanding your *why* can assign authentic purpose to your life. Why you work is entirely your choice. Get engaged with choosing, not just accepting what is.

HOW YOU WORK

How you deliver each aspect of your business is the final component of engaging with the business development and happiness-creation process in your practice. Business systems and processes comprise a big part of running an efficient and effective practice. But like the other five elements we've discussed, so many healthcare practices aren't actively engaged with creating effective and efficient systems – and processes to support them. Before we look more closely at your *systems* and *processes*, let's get clear on the difference between the two.

A *system* is an overarching way of achieving something. For example, you have a system for service delivery – how you deliver your clinical services each day. That system is broken down into processes that collectively give you the desired end result.

Then, within your system of delivering clinical services, you have *processes*. These include things like preparing the room, running the clinical session, scheduling return appointments, following up with patients, etc. Your processes create your system.

All small businesses need systems and processes in the following areas:

- Finance
- Business future planning
- People management
- Customer service delivery
- Business development
- Marketing and sales
- Continuous improvement

And within each of these areas you have both systems and processes. That is, you have overarching ways of doing things and step-by-step elements that ensure the system runs as effectively and efficiently as possible.

There may not immediately appear to be a direct connection between systems, processes, and your happiness in your business – but there is.

Efficient and effective systems and processes can make your life inside your business run much more smoothly, which in turn can positively impact how you feel about the business.

Sadly, the road to establishing and implementing effective systems and processes isn't necessarily one that many practitioners enjoy. That said, you can always delegate or outsource the process of establishing your internal operating systems, if that's something you want and can fund. You will likely have multiple systems in each area of your practice. For example, under finance, you could have systems related to:

- New patients' pre-payment
- Automatic billing for repeat purchases
- Invoice payments
- Reviewing weekly cashflow reports
- Chasing bad debt, etc.

For each of these systems, multiple processes consistently support the system working. The processes that support your systems in these areas can include automated or software-driven and manual, human actions.

Technology has enabled us to streamline many tasks like the issuing of receipts, taking regular payments, stock control, posting on social media, monitoring sales revenue, reminding patients of appointments etc. There are so many technology-driven systems now that just keeping up with the latest ones can be a challenge for small practice owners. But you must do just that to maximise your efficiencies.

On the flipside, the human actions needed to complete specific processes within your systems require documenting, training or mentoring, and reviewing and changing on a regular basis. Most practices find the best way to do this is by establishing specific written and/or video-based instructions to ensure the task is repeated the same, every single time, with no element missed. This ensures quality, repeatable actions that get the job done in the most effective and efficient way every time.

Documenting the process isn't sufficient on its own. Just because you have a documented system for call answering, for example, doesn't mean it will be delivered effectively. Systems also must be established to ensure new team members are taught and supported through the process of learning the business systems! Adequate training, supervision, reviews, and support are essential for you and your team to deliver your systems and processes consistently.

This might all feel pretty tedious and like a lot of hard work. Deciding how to run your business isn't a simple task, but going through this process early in business's life will make things so much easier down the line. Creating systems and processes is a brilliant example of short-term pain for long-term gain. The pain is very definitely worth the effort. Ultimately, how you work in your practice is entirely your choice. Get engaged with choosing, not just accepting what is.

CONCLUSION

Hopefully you can see the influence you have over your happiness and positivity in your practice, if you spend time developing each of the six happiness factors.

This can feel like a lot of hard work to intentionally choose how each of these areas will operate inside your practice. But if you truly want to be happy in your business, you must take on this challenge and identify how you want to apply each element. Then, work at building your version of each element into your practice. Yes, it takes time, and yes, it takes energy – but the payback at the end of this engagement process will be real and hugely positive.

ACTION POINTS TO ENSURE YOU ENGAGED

☐ Choose who you work with

☐ Choose where you work

☐ Choose what you 'sell'

☐ Create a Patient Referral Network

☐ Complete Decluttering exercise

YOU'RE NOW ENGAGED √

NOTES

FLOOR 4 – VALUE:

Understanding Your Worth as a Healthcare Professional

√ Value and worth aren't the same.

√ There are different money personalities.

√ Think beyond your own business.

√ You don't need to undercharge to prove yourself.

Do any of these statements ring true to you?:

- *I can't afford that (expensive) piece of equipment for my business.*
- *Taking time off for courses costs me money.*
- *My clients wouldn't pay more to see me.*
- *I don't want to charge my patients more.*

If so, then this is the floor for you. In it, we'll explore some important concepts that are frequently overlooked in our business plans. Neglecting these can cost us, our businesses, and our patients dearly.

VALUE AND WORTH

Knowing our value is an emotional subject, and most professionals are often confused when asked about it. It's much easier to know when we don't feel valued, respected, or appreciated, but individually knowing our value is quite different. It involves sensing your own value as a professional and understanding how much of a difference you've made in any given situation. If you look, you will see your value in so many situations in your field, where your actions and presence made a significant difference.

Value and *worth* are often used interchangeably, but their distinct differences may help you as a private healthcare professional. Let's explore their definitions:

WORTH:
The actual cost of something — i.e., what it costs or sells for.

VALUE:
What something is worth to someone — i.e., variable and influenced by emotion.

Your worth relates to the fees you charge for the services in your business. There will be a cost of providing your services, which can be calculated from analysis of your business overheads as follows:

- Premises costs (rent/mortgage, rates, utilities, insurances)
- Staff costs (clinician, administrator, manager, ancillary – even if all carried out by the healthcare professional [HCP] themselves)
- On-costs (additional statutory costs related to staff – sick leave, annual leave, taxes, etc.)
- Equipment costs (to provide your services, including servicing and replacement of such)
- Stock costs (to provide your services, but cost could also be recouped from sales of such)
- Training costs (for all staff in your business to provide existing and new services)
- Outsource costs (for tasks not carried out within your business, such as accountancy, legal services)

By totalling all of these cost categories and factoring in the number of clients seen and services offered, a unit cost can be established. Businesses that base the worth of their services on that calculation won't go as far wrong. All of their overheads will be covered, providing they can achieve and sustain the factored-in numbers.

This is the basis of *cost-based pricing*, where the business is the focus. However, healthcare professionals often struggle with these factors when setting their fees. Instead of the logically-processed figures for fees – achieved from these listed calculations – they introduce value into their decision-making. This creates *market-based pricing*, also known as *value-based*. In this model, the business determines how much value it will generate for the customer through, for example, cost-savings, patient experience, happiness/satisfaction, consistency, and safety.

Pricing is ultimately reinforced by customer demand and expectations. Some patients may be alienated if they aren't willing to pay your prices.

The drawback of value-based pricing occurs when healthcare professionals fail to realise that value is individually determined and based on emotion. In an attempt to "normalise" personal biases generated by what they feel the value of services are, providers compare their fees to other providers of similar services. This misses the very important part, which is the value of to patients of the individual providers themselves, and that's not so readily comparable.

The damaging result of this is that the providers then feel scared to change that approach to fee-setting, and they develop beliefs that reinforce that fear. How often have you said or heard other healthcare professionals say, "My patients wouldn't pay that" or "They all moan when I raise my fees, so I don't do it as much/often as I should." These insecurities about pricing aren't real to everyone, just to those who have also used the *comparable fees* approach to their business.

So why do we set our fees in line with others based on historical fee levels? There will be many possible reasons, not the least of which is because we haven't understood the difference between worth and value. See if your mindset regarding value and worth change after reading this next example.

Dear Jill – What's the Difference Between Value and Worth in Private Healthcare?

We have all experienced pain due to a health-related problem. On one end of the scale, we may have a temporary, low-intensity headache. On the other end of the same scale, we may have a vomit-inducing migraine that seems never-ending. On the surface, one of those appears to be much worse than the other – with much more of an *impact on life quality. Any solution to ease the physical pain and its effects would seem to be worth more* for the migraine than for the headache. Indeed, the cost of the different drugs to treat each condition reflects that difference – with paracetamol (a common treatment for headaches) costing pennies, and erenumab (an advanced medication for migraine) costing thousands of pounds.*

But if we delve deeper, each story could reveal the opposite to be true, because pain is complex, and emotional pain can actually be more than physical pain. So in our example, the person with the headache may have planned to spend the day with their grandchildren, on their annual visit from abroad. They've spent every day from their last visit looking forward to their next one. They've spent days, weeks. or even months planning for the day ahead. They've bought expensive tickets for an amazing, shared experience with their loved ones. It's their best day of the year, yet they've woken up with a headache. The pain isn't that bad but it's distracting. It's affecting their mood, and that could then affect the interactions with their grandchildren. They don't want anything to spoil the day, as they know it's their only chance to create wonderful memories to last all year until their next visit. So now, how much is the headache medication worth to them*? Would they pay more for it?

*Humans tend to get lazy with the use of language, which then muddies the waters of understanding. Instead of "be worth more" this should really read "have more value"; and instead of' "worth to them" it should say "value to them." It's the individual perspective that defines value, but worth is defined by the actual cost to develop, produce, and supply the medication.

WE'RE ALL DIFFERENT

Why do some people see more value in things than others? The answer lies in the variability of human personalities. In the medication example, some would indeed pay more for the lower cost intervention; some wouldn't. Some would pay as much as the migraine drug, thousands; some would pay even more.

We have no way of knowing how someone values the products and services they receive without getting to know them better, including understanding their own money values. That's because we'd all make different decisions in the same circumstances, as we each have different upbringings, influences, values, and goals. This concept applies to any new client that engages with our business. We have no idea what personality we're dealing with in that initial interaction (which may include them looking on our website, messaging us, placing a telephone conversation, or seeing us in person).

Many internet resources talk about six different money personalities. Laird Norton, a wealth management firm in Seattle, uses the following descriptions when looking at their clients and approach to finances:

THE SAVER

- You take pride in saving rather than spending.
- You enjoy watching your savings grow.
- You'd rather not buy something than risk paying too much for it.
- You frequently choose less over more.
- You can spend money but get more satisfaction from having money left over.
- You may find it hard to treat yourself or even spend on essentials.
- You may have trouble being generous with others.
- You could miss out on valuable opportunities and experiences.

Note for savers: Money is a means to an end, not an end in itself.

THE SPENDER

- You don't agonize over spending money.
- You love to give gifts.
- You spend money as soon as it's available.
- You have a "live for today" attitude.
- You tend to see a deal in every transaction.
- You know a good deal when you see it.
- Your spare cash goes to things that give pleasure to you and those you care about.
- You may have trouble saving and controlling your debt.
- You may put too much emphasis on status.
- Your self-worth could depend too much on material things.

Note for spenders: Saving and giving can feel just as good as spending.

THE SECURITY SEEKER

- You like to play it safe.
- Before spending money, you must feel you've explored all the options.
- You don't like to borrow or lend money.
- You spend money but get more satisfaction from adding to your savings.
- You may overthink things.
- You may have difficulty ceasing opportunities or being spontaneous.
- You may become overly focused on yourself.

Note for security seekers: Open up! Take some risks! Doing well means doing good for yourself and your community.

THE RISK TAKER

- You tend to have an all-or-nothing mentality.
- You tend to see a deal in every transaction.

- You like to negotiate.
- You think a big potential payoff makes a calculated risk worthwhile.
- You'd rather invest than save money.
- You may need help setting limits when it comes to financial transactions.
- You may become impatient and gloss over risks and problems.
- You may end up losing money.

Note for risk takers: Slow down! Take time to assess what can go wrong before you dive in.

THE GIVER

- You focus on and enjoy helping others.
- You're generous with your own time and money.
- You feel responsible for others' well-being.
- Putting yourself first is hard to do.
- You may have a hard time saying no.
- You may ignore your self-interest.
- You do a lot of wishful thinking.

Note for givers: Take care of yourself first, then serve others.

THE FLYER

- Money matters are of no interest to you.
- You like to explore, have new experiences.
- You're generous with your time and money.
- Planning ahead seems like a drag.
- Lack of planning could cause problems.
- You may be too quick to give control of your money to others who don't act in your best interest.
- You may end up living beyond your means.

Note for flyers: Taking good care of my money allows me to do what I want.

From our experience of running many workshops and giving talks on fees and money, there are lots of crossover personalities that create many more different types. The important thing to remember is that our own money personality may not match any of our clients. Therefore, we shouldn't make decisions for others based on our own money values.

Yet so many private healthcare professionals seem to do just that. For instance, if you're careful with money, do you project that onto your patients, so that you're careful with their money as well? Perhaps you buy items based on cost more than quality (or vice versa) and think your patients should too. Effectively, you end up making financial decisions for them. The decisions can be direct, such as "I wouldn't spend my money on that," or indirect, such as not offering some treatment options based on your own biases. Those decisions are yours, not your patients', so they aren't empowered or in control of their own actions. This can have a detrimental effect on your relationship with them and your business.

IS MY WORTH AS A HEALTHCARE PROVIDER DIFFERENT TO MY VALUE?

Having established the difference between value and worth, and having clarified how that distinction is applied to our businesses and the services we offer, now it gets complicated. From the earlier explanation, it seemed like value was individual (and therefore variable from person to person and time to time), whereas worth was more structured based on costs or selling price. However, generally humans do attribute value to the "greatness" of a person, and all too often this comes from how others perceive us, rather than how we perceive ourselves.

Perceiving ourselves in a good light and having a positive mental attitude is so important to our businesses.

If we don't think we're sufficiently *great*, then how can we expect our patients to think so? If we allow negative comments to knock us down and we internalise criticism, then our self-esteem will suffer, and we won't be confident in providing our services or growing our business. The problem is that once again, we fall into the trap of comparing ourselves to others, especially those who we perceive as "greater" than us. We think that we can't possibly be worth as much as them, because they have more knowledge or skills – or are more able or confident than we are.

You may have heard of this; it's called *imposter syndrome*. It's detrimental to our self-esteem and stops us from fulfilling our potential. We may even compare our own profession to other professions, and then the healthcare industry to other industries. This can lead to negative and restrictive thoughts about what we're capable of, either as individuals or collectively, which influences our beliefs and behaviours.

However, we can overcome such thoughts by looking at how the public values their own health, health problems, and health solution providers – such as private healthcare professionals.

"HEALTH IS WEALTH" – OR IS IT?

Our worth as a healthcare professional is quite difficult to quantify. Yet we must know our worth to our clients. We must challenge ourselves to *do more* to *be worth more*. We must talk about health – and the healthcare industry – in detail.

To understand the phrase "health is wealth," we should check out the individual meaning and importance of both words. According to the World Health Organization (WHO), *health* is defined as "a state of complete physical, mental, and social well-being and not merely the absence of disease and infirmity." Just because our body is free of disease doesn't mean we're healthy. Also, environmental fitness is a crucial part of health. A healthy environment is necessary in every aspect of life to avoid persistent exposure to health-diminishing diseases.

Health:
Fitness of the body or mind and freedom from disease or ailment.

Wealth:
A great quantity of money, valuable possessions, property, or other riches.

It's sad that many people have failed to realise that health is the true wealth. We can live without wealth, but without health it's difficult to thrive or even survive. It's only when we're healthy that we can earn wealth. But if we're wealthy and caught by a deadly or chronic disease – because of not considering our health as priority – our wealth will be of no use. There are frequent news stories of financially-comfortable celebrities dying of cancer, for instance. Their wealth didn't stop the inevitable.

It's a pity that so many put a much greater price on wealth than anything. They often work very hard for wealth, thinking that it's hard to catch. People put so much effort into finding the sources of riches, without realising the internal stress that keeps building up day by day. These stress levels increase until one day, possibly with an immense collapse/breakdown, we realise that in all this frantic activity, we've overlooked caring for one important thing – our health. In the race to collect wealth, we often forget the major concept about the real value of the world, and that's that health *is* wealth – and the most essential wealth at that.

Some people have different views. Some believe that wealth is everything, because it can buy attractive houses, classy cars, fashionable shoes, and beautiful clothes. Some even assume that money can buy them more life and spiritual happiness.

We disagree, believing that *health is wealth* itself, because without health, it's difficult to enjoy life. Without health, how can we appreciate the beauty of each day and acknowledge the delights that come to even the meekest encounters with family and friends? Without health, no one could work productively. Therefore, the opportunities for earning and making money would be slim. To generate income, most of us must work, and that cannot be done if we're ill and unable to engage in income-generating activities.

So, in conclusion, health is very necessary for generating wealth – and therefore, it is wealth. Hence the need to make people realise that good health should be one of the most important priorities. Educating patients on the value of their health is one of our major tasks as healthcare professionals, and one that we often don't realise or understand.

THE WIDER WORLD VIEW

Health has always been a major factor determining the productivity, standard of living, and growth of the economy of any country. Healthcare systems can either be managed by governments or private organisations. It's the responsibility of these organisations to ensure that their healthcare providers provide valuable service. This requires confronting, further training, or even barring unsafe practitioners from patient care.

Public healthcare is usually provided by the government through national healthcare systems, while private healthcare can be provided via private hospitals/clinics or not-for-profit, non-government providers or self-employed practitioners. Of these, public health professionals and public health organisations focus on the health needs of the entire population or population groups. They address health issues through outreach, health education, and provision of services. Private healthcare professionals, on the other hand, may be more efficient and responsive to patient needs because of market competition. They may be able to overcome government inefficiency and even corruption.

The margin between a developing and developed country is defined by their progress in healthcare. A strong healthcare sector correlates with a lower death rate and higher level of life expectancy, which largely influences the growth and development of any economy. Hence, it's critical that a country takes good care of its healthcare sector – catering to its population effectively and contributing to the country's positive growth index.

The inability of those on lower income to pay for private services is one of the major reasons governments advocate for public health. Private healthcare providers have little incentive to consider population-based services, although they may provide individual clinical preventative care. Even with increased attention on providing clinical preventative services by managed care organisations and others, in the private sector, the clinical preventative services often are those with short-range, immediate payoffs.

Private healthcare professionals are closer to their patients, because they're more versatile and readily available than government healthcare.

Despite this statement, it's quite unfortunate that over time, many patients take these providers for granted, and their value is sometimes not fully appreciated. Our value as a healthcare professional in society is possibly more complex than we imagine. We're responsible for educating and enlightening people on the need to take their health seriously.

People tend to invest and spend more on frivolities and things that will even endanger their health than on paying for private healthcare to keep them healthy. However, one of our major duties that reflects our value in society is to change their mindset. We're responsible for making sure the health and well-being of our patients are optimal.

REACHING THE PUBLIC AND GAINING THEIR LOYALTY

Modern technologies can help communities to achieve better health, as they improve communication and feedback from the patient to the practitioner and vice versa. They also provide a range of opportunities for educating the public about their health and the solutions we provide. A lot of businesses and start-ups have gone digital, and many professionals are now leveraging the evolution of the internet to promote their products and services.

A very important tool used in this process is social media, where you can now easily sell your worth as a private healthcare professional. Social media has become a part of the lives of hundreds of millions of people around the world. Interestingly, the healthcare industry, which is one of the largest industries in the world, has proven to be no exception to this rule. As these trends continue evolving, you must see yourself riding the wave of new social media practices. Challenge yourself to do more, so people can see why they need your services.

Social media makes it easier for us to offer value up front, developing a *know-like-trust* relationship with our potential customers. Posting regular valuable information such as online resources and videos, etc. can help establish you as the go-to person with solutions for patients' problems, even before they become your patients.

As a business owner, you get to decide how you want to run things. This means that your healthcare business can and should be different to the one down the road or in the next town. It should reflect your own personal and professional values, whilst not being limited by your own self-imposed blocks to success. If you ever hear yourself saying, "I can't do that because...," then you really must explore if the rest of the sentence is a fact or belief (see Floor 2).

As healthcare professionals, we may think that our patients want the exact treatment plans that improve outcomes. However, patients are also interested in more than compassion and clinical expertise. Patients of today want more personalised services. They want a professional who is engaged in their healthcare, understanding of their busy lifestyles, and easy to reach.

According to "The Patient-Provider Relationship Study" by SolutionReach in 2017 (https://www.solutionreach.com/rethinking-thepatient-provider-relationship n.d.), which is based on a survey of nearly 2,100 patients ages twenty-one to seventy, all patients want four key things from their physicians:

1. Greater connectivity
2. Convenience (for example, via text)
3. Online tools
4. More time with their doctors

From this study, striving to meet patients' ideals isn't just a noble endeavour – it's a necessity. Exploring these factors can give healthcare businesses a better understanding of the most effective ways to improve patient satisfaction and loyalty.

Few situations are as frustrating for patients as not being able to reach their private healthcare professionals when they need medical attention. A way to improve connectivity is to leverage different communication mediums such as emails, phones, and texts, so that your patients can communicate with you and your colleagues, make appointments, or pay bills. Asking and answering simple questions through those communication channels will have a positive effect on patients' experiences. The same holds true for letting patients schedule or change their own appointments. These tools will empower patients, promote communication, and increase your value to them. However, make sure that whichever tools you use (such as text reminders and confirmations) actually benefit both the patient and the business. Otherwise repeated errors or problems can cause the patient to become disengaged from the business.

Online tools such as e-newsletters can help professionals respond to patients' issues. Branded mailshots/e-blasts can inform patients about new treatments, remind them when it's time for a check-up, and provide trusted resources and information about how to spot budding health issues.

A growing number of patients also prefer to receive appointment reminders and other information via secure text messages. Unlike calls, which require patients to interrupt what they're doing to engage in conversation, texting makes receiving and responding to notifications easy; patients can do it anytime, anywhere, at their convenience. Private healthcare professionals can easily accommodate this patient preference using automated text reminders, follow-up reminders, patient confirmations, and last-minute scheduling notifications using automated tools.

One of the biggest complaints among patients is that they don't get as much time with their healthcare professionals as they would like, especially in a public health setting. Though it might be difficult for us to find more time due to our workload and number of patients to attend to, in our private businesses, we still must find more time to spend with patients. Listening to and learning from them will help us meet and exceed their expectations.

HEALTH PROBLEM-SOLVERS

Our patients typically present to us with at least one problem, of which they have an expectation for the outcome. For us to satisfy that expectation, we must go through a five-step process:

1. Vision
2. Analysis
3. Process
4. Solution
5. Success

First, we have to define what we and our businesses can deliver to the public. This is the *business vision*. This includes what the patient experience will look like, what services we offer, and how we'll manage the patient as a person, not just a condition. Then there's the *analysis*, which is where the patient starts to tell you about their specific problem(s). Essentially it's the history-taking. This should take place before the *process* of assessing the patient's problem(s). We then come up with the *solution*, which involves treatment and/ or advice. This hopefully leads to resolution of the problem(s) – and *success*. Integral to this process are our knowledge, tools, skills, and abilities to be problem-solvers.

> The more of these tools and skills we bring to the table, the more competent we can be in achieving our patients' expectations.

It's important for not only our businesses, but for ourselves, to grow in what we can provide for our patients.

UNDERSTANDING YOUR VALUE TO PATIENTS

One of your patients' main reasons for seeking a private healthcare business is the range of services that they can offer. The same services may not be available to patients in public healthcare. Even if they are, the referral and justification processes within the public system can be exhaustive before a patient even qualifies for the treatment – especially when they're in a hierarchical competition with others for the resources that public healthcare can offer. Those resources include staff, facilities, equipment, appointment availability, etc.

Therefore, as a private healthcare professional, this is one of your selling points. You can offer treatments based upon the individual's needs, not limited by resources, and you can address your patients' pain points effectively and efficiently.

Further understanding of your value to patients occurs when you realise that you're essential to all people who need the healthcare you provide. You're expected to help people in a variety of different ways, such as keeping close records of your patient's medical history and treating them when they become ill or are injured.

You'll be responsible to diagnose – to determine if they have a problem or are developing some type of condition that could negatively impact their lives. You can even extend your services and become a family healthcare provider, where you're involved in the treatment of a whole family. In essence, the main benefit of private healthcare is that you have the time and space to give your clients the level of attention, expertise, and service they deserve.

For many, now may be an ideal time to convince them why they need a private healthcare professional like you. It could be the most important investment of their lives.

YOUR WORTH IS A MINDSET THING

Some healthcare professionals have been in healthcare for so many years, yet they aren't aware of their value.

You might be smart, technical, creative, and innovative in how you offer your services to your patients. But not knowing your own value might make others overlook your achievement. Without embracing your value and worth, you may lack confidence and awareness of your crucial role as a healthcare professional. Ultimately, as the owner, it's your responsibility to develop a successful business. Doing so impacts your future as well as your patients' lives, so your confidence is crucial.

Here are some key components of *self* that you can work on to make a massive difference:

- Exhibiting positive self-esteem
- Making a difference and recognising it
- Seeing yourself as a peer
- Not undercharging for your services
- Being clear about your value

EXHIBITING POSITIVE SELF-ESTEEM

Self-esteem is confidence in one's own worth or abilities. When you believe in and like yourself for who you're – your weight, height, and everything that makes and represents you – that's self-esteem. When you're confident in the work you deliver, your great relationship with your patients, and your sense of professionalism, you'll easily see your value. However, without positive self-esteem, knowing your value will remain difficult.

MAKING A DIFFERENCE AND RECOGNISING IT

When you know your value, you'll confidently approach a negotiation with full belief in your knowledge, skills, and experience – and the difference you can make. For example, if you diagnosed a patient and let them know the nature of their problem through your assessment, you'll feel confident prescribing the required treatment plan.

Part of this involves being sure of what your assessment results mean. If you're confident, your professionalism throughout the diagnosis process will project onto your patient. Your value will be noticed and respected. You'll also be happy for the impact made when your patient improves based on your assessment and treatment plan, especially if they've been in pain for a long time.

SEEING YOURSELF AS A PEER

In any given situation, knowing your value means feeling that you're an equal with anyone with whom you interact: patients, colleagues, public professionals, doctors, nurses, or surgeons. If you always have a personal sense of value and deservedness, and you assert yourself as an equal with your patients by trying to put yourself in their shoes, you'll be able to see the real value in yourself.

NOT UNDERCHARGING FOR YOUR SERVICES

One of the greatest mistakes made by most professionals (especially allied health professionals – those allied to medicine) is undercharging for services. When undercharging for your services, you're not only losing funds, but you're also diminishing your worth and value.

Often, the fear of losing out on business, or the desire to win more business in the future, makes professionals undercharge. As a private healthcare professional, this creates a bad situation, because you end doing much more than you're paid to do.

You don't need to undercharge to prove yourself. You will continually be unhappy with yourself if you do so consistently.

BE CLEAR ABOUT YOUR VALUE

Sometimes you must clearly state your value for your patients, instead of just hoping they understand it. Some of your patients may want to assume you're just like other healthcare professionals. Once you're clear about who you are, how you like to be treated and spoken to, and how much you charge for your services – and you also have the courage to speak out when necessary – you don't need anyone's validation to prove your value. Once you have that self-value, it's easier to make some authoritative decisions such as negotiating, saying no, facing conflict, engaging in relationships, among so many others.

However, do not let your self-importance and value control you. The belief and mindset that *only you can do something perfectly* is dangerous. In the end, you'll find out you don't have time for your personal life and family – but you also may ostracize or detriment your patients. For example, there are so many healthcare professionals working, even when they are also not feeling fine. This isn't good for anyone. Not taking care of yourself at the expense of other people is a mistaken view of self-importance.

Some professionals believe that they must always be there to make things work in their businesses. They see themselves as *survival* for the patients, thinking that their partners and colleagues won't cope if they're not there. They think the whole world will stop working if they're away for a day. These people have forgotten that life continues when they're dead. Tragically, this belief is coupled with low self-value, rather than a genuine belief in their own worth. This can work to an extreme. When someone feels like they're the only ones who can effectively provide a service, they may neglect to treat a patient with kindness, instead defaulting to arrogance.

We should understand our worth, but also humbly realise that others also have worth. We must always earn the business we deliver, despite our confidence.

MANAGING CAREER DISAPPOINTMENTS

Unfortunately, there will be times in your professional career when things don't go to plan, and you'll disappoint yourself and/or others. You may be tempted to doubt your worth. Disappointment is natural in a healthcare profession's career. How you respond to it is what matters.

When you experience a career setback – such as redundancy, lack of promotion, or even just negative feedback/reviews – and it creates a negative impact on you personally, you might want to take some time for self-care in order to recover emotionally. Sometimes, all it might take is hanging out with family or friends. Sometimes, a week-long (or month-long!) holiday from work may help you get over it. Or you may need to set a boundary in some area of your life – or with someone.

It is said that nothing is better than a good relationship. But also, nothing is worse than a bad one. If you feel you might be dejected or hurt by a certain set of friends or a family member, it might be wise to avoid them. The same applies to patients. You can't please all the people all the time, and you don't need assaults on your self-value. So it's perfectly acceptable for you to refuse to see patients who may be a risk to your own self-esteem. Instead, surround yourself with those who help you feel that your self-value is fed.

If you still don't feel loved and secure after a disappointment, you might consider also working briefly with a good life/career wellness coach. Taking time for yourself can help you recover emotionally more quickly. Using a journal can be helpful to sort out your feelings, and it can also be healing. You must ask yourself questions – such as how you feel about the career disappointment – to help you focus. As caregivers, we're sometimes too focussed on giving to others and forget to give to ourselves. We tend to remain in the role of healer and fixer, when sometimes we're the ones who need healing and our own attention.

Spending time communing with nature is also a good strategy for overcoming disappointment or battered esteem. Walking in a forest, park, or even your own garden can provide mindfulness in an environment that's healthy and free of work stress, allowing your brain a crucial break. Taking care of yourself physically will help you heal. If you comfort-eat when you feel stressed, you might want to try drinking more water, which can help to fill you up, keep you hydrated, and eliminate toxins. In addition, proper exercise can help release endorphins that increase an overall feeling of well-being.

You're the only one who can make yourself happy; your happiness depends on you. Whichever way you may choose to heal from the emotional impact of a healthcare career disappointment, viewing it as a *setback* rather than a personal *failure* may help you recover more quickly.

DON'T GIVE UP

When your patients put you under pressure, how do you feel? Do you find yourself giving up more often than pushing through the difficulties? Do you challenge yourself by saying, *I can do better*? In that moment, it often may seem like the easiest solution is to let the situation control you, as you move on to something different. However, don't sell yourself short of your true potential, when you simply don't have the energy or capacity to push through challenges. You must see through this situation – to a better outcome.

Challenging yourself to always exceed your expectations is beneficial not only to your mental health, but also to your personal well-being. As you conquer challenges that stand in your way – like roadblocks, refusing to allow your passing – your confidence grows. Confidence is such an important characteristic on the path to success.

When you find yourself in a difficult situation, the worst thing to do is to give up. You must keep pushing to the end. A failure once isn't a failure for life. Giving up on any given task because of the difficulties that fall before you means giving up on yourself. When you give up on yourself, you lose faith in your skills, knowledge, and even career, which consequently leads to a lower self-esteem.

If you continue to battle through life's hardships, find solutions to problems, and focus on putting those solutions into effect, you'll find satisfaction in your efforts. It's so important to maintain a high level of self-esteem, believe in yourself, and continue to challenge yourself in order to build upon your knowledge in all that you do.

Next time you see a challenge in front of you, face it. Challenge yourself and prove that you're capable of achieving anything. While there are times when a challenge is a sign that a bigger change in direction is needed, often these are merely roadblocks that you must detour around on your path to success.

If you don't believe in yourself, how can you expect your patients to believe in you? How can you convince them they must take care of their health? How can you make them realise their health is wealth? With confidence in yourself and your work comes the reward of others' confidence in you. Fuelling that confidence is growing self-value, which results from tackling challenges.

WHAT SHOULD MY FEES BE?

As you assess your value and worth, eventually you'll consider what you should charge your patients. Your fees are individual to you and your business, but they shouldn't be set to attract all customers. They should be set to cover all the costs of the business – including an allowance for growth – whilst enabling you to enjoy your working day as fully as possible and provide for your future.

They shouldn't be limited by your beliefs, but guided by facts gained from valid information sources, including your own data. The longer established your business is, the more data you'll have to make use of; but the more skewed the data will be towards the full range of patients, rather than just your ideal patients.

Remember that colleagues (local and sometimes further afield) may use your fees as a guideline for setting their fees, so your fees will have a greater significance beyond your business to your wider profession. Don't be limited by fear, but exchange your value for your patients' money. Educate them as to the value of investing in their health – and why you and your business represent the place for that investment.

EXERCISE
The Value Proposition

This exercise will help you to think outside the box when it comes to your fees, assessing where you may be charging less than you could for services you deliver (or could add to your offerings).

STEP 1: Take one of your fee levels (for example, your new patient fee).

STEP 2: Multiply it by at least ten.

STEP 3: Write down that amount in large letters at the top of a piece of paper and underline it.

STEP 4: Create a package of your services that will deliver that amount of value to a patient. Include all things that make up the overall patient experience – even things such as a meet-and-greet, refreshments, etc.

STEP 5: Now start removing those services that aren't essential to address the patient's problem(s).

STEP 6: Then look at the remaining services in the package. These are the essential ones to solve the patient's problem(s).

STEP 7: Re-price those essential services to achieve the fee figure you wrote down at the top of the page.

For example, let's say you have a new patient consultation fee of £100. If you multiply that by 10, you get £1,000. To deliver that amount of value to a patient, you may consider that you need all of the following:

- Engaging and informative website
- Simple online booking of an appointment to suit (same day if necessary)
- Personalised response with phone call from you
- Gold-embossed welcome letter hand delivered by you
- Complimentary chauffeur-driven limousine to take patient to and from their appointment
- Champagne on arrival at the most amazing-looking state-of-the-art clinic
- Massage chairs with personal music choice in waiting area
- Waiter/waitress service for refreshments
- Welcome greeting by the clinic owner
- A two-hour appointment with the highest-qualified clinician involving:
    - holistic health checks
    - computerised in-depth assessments
    - presentation folder of findings and reports
    - accurate diagnosis of the presenting problem(s)
    - thorough advice/treatment
    - addressing of any other issues found during the assessments
    - personalised video feedback
    - daily review video calls until desired clinical outcome has been met.

Do you think you'd be able to charge £1,000 for all that, rather than £100? Now if we remove the services that aren't essential to address the patient's problem(s), we're left with in-depth assessments, accurate diagnosis, thorough advice and treatment, and review (giving us five services in total).

So, this new higher fee of £1,000 is what you could charge to solve your patient's issue(s), and they would still be satisfied with the outcome. Those five services could be charged at £200 each (priced equally for ease in this example), whereas before they were charged at £100 in total (effectively £20 each, if applied equally). Therefore, to achieve the new higher fee, each "service" has had a 900 percent fee increase. Next, you add back in the non-essential services you most want from those you removed. Consider what additional benefit they bring to the patient, as well as the cost of providing those services, and charge accordingly for them – allowing for those that help you deliver your WOW (see Floor 5).

You've now rewritten your fee structure based on the value to your patient. This value proposition exercise can be repeated for different packages of services to help you explore the potential value of what you offer. All you need to do then is to market those packages to attract patients who will want them, which we will cover on the next floor.

If you don't believe this works and the higher fees aren't achievable, just look at your local private hospital and the fees they're charging to resolve their patient's problems. You will be surprised!

ACTION POINTS TO ENSURE YOU KNOW YOUR VALUE

☐ Understand money personalities

☐ Understand your value and of the solutions you provide

☐ Exhibit positive self-esteem

☐ Make a difference and recognise it

☐ See yourself as a peer

☐ Don't undercharge

☐ Be clear about your value

☐ Don't give up

☐ Complete The Value Proposition exercise

YOU NOW KNOW YOUR VALUE √

NOTES

FLOOR 5 — ACTION:

Marketing and Advertising
in the Digital Age

- √ People need you.
- √ Don't copy others who are unsuccessful at marketing.
- √ Follow the essential ingredients.
- √ Marketing is a long game.
- √ Focus on your dream patient.
- √ Know your value statement.

We see many healthcare practices whose marketing activity is built on the flimsiest of foundations. By that, we mean that the practitioners don't know what marketing actually is, don't know how it works or how to measure its effect, and are mostly using the *fire and pray* method. That is, they fire off random promotional activities and pray something works. This isn't the strategy of action you need if you want to build a thriving profitable practice.

This floor won't teach you how to create your personal brand or use Instagram. Nor will it show you how to structure your website or develop your referral network. You've got Google and YouTube to teach you that stuff. That's not the action we're talking about. What we want for our readers is to help them elevate themselves well above their local competitors. And the way we can do that, while building real resilience into your marketing, is by teaching you how marketing works. Then you can build yours on a strong foundation.

THE TRUTH ABOUT MARKETING

Marketing often sits in the *too difficult* box within the minds of healthcare practitioners. Or it lies in the part of their brain that cringes and turns off the lights when thinking about selling anything. So, we want to get two things on the table before we start.

First, marketing isn't easy, and it's currently moving at one heck of a speed as technology takes us all on a bit of a rollercoaster ride. But it can be simple, and often simple can be the most effective. We're not promising that this floor will lift marketing firmly out of the *too difficult* box. But hopefully by the end, you'll feel more empowered to start making informed decisions and taking baby steps forwards.

Second, let's talk about the reputation of marketing. It's really sad that marketing has received unnecessary bad press for being sleazy, pushy, salesy, and cheesy. Unfortunately, second-hand car salesmen, cold callers, spam e-mails, pay-day loan companies, and betting agencies have definitely dirtied the water when it comes to the reputation of marketing.

While these things all happen, this reputation is a shame, because marketing can be the rocket fuel your practice needs. We genuinely believe that marketing is one of the most ethical tools you can use in your healthcare practice. Let us explain.

Outside of your practice, in your local community, there are a sea of people in pain. They are in physical and emotional pain and uncertain about where to turn for help. If you do a poor job with your marketing – if you keep quiet and pretend that you're not really selling anything, only reaching out to help in a quiet or apologetic way – you're doing all of those people in pain a massive disservice. How will they ever figure out that your profession – and you in particular, in their local area – have the answers to give them back their quality of life?

It's your duty as a trained healthcare professional to get good at this. Understand marketing, so that you can reach out and help as many people as possible in your local community.

PEOPLE NEED YOU!
But they won't find you or understand how you can help unless you get really good at marketing.

BUT MARKETING DOESN'T WORK!

Once we've got people over the hump of feeling repulsed by the thought of marketing their practice and selling their services, the next barrier we often face as coaches is when practitioners tell us that marketing doesn't work.

That's often based on a sample of one! That's right. They have a sample size of one practice, where they didn't know what they were doing. As it turns out, they had copied the practice down the road (who incidentally also didn't know what they were doing). They tried something for a week and a half, but because there wasn't a stampede of new patients into their clinic, they decided that marketing didn't work.

The most common reasons we see that marketing isn't working for health practitioners are:

- They are trained clinicians with no training in marketing, so they don't know what they're doing.
- They are copying other practices where the practitioners also don't know what they're doing.
- They have no clear strategy and are just using a scattergun approach.
- They aren't consistent – with their target audience, messaging, branding, or marketing content output.

The problem is that most practice owners were trained as clinicians, not as marketing professionals. So how and why would they know how marketing works? They don't see marketing as something that takes time to understand and dedication to apply in a way that works in their industry and location. Instead, they watch a YouTube video on how to post on Twitter, claim their Google My Business profile, and get someone (who probably doesn't understand healthcare or healthcare marketing) to build them a website. Then, they think that their marketing is done – when in reality, this is like printing a business card and doing nothing with it. The material may be created, but marketing involves making sure the right people see and engage with it. That's oversimplifying the reality, but hopefully you get the point.

Remember how you studied for years to understand and be great at your clinical role? Well – spoiler alert – all of those marketing graduates also studied for years. Marketing is a huge subject (which crazily, we're about to try and boil down to one floor in this book!). It takes time to understand and apply marketing practices to get them working for you.

So all we ask is that you approach this floor with an open mind and excitement for what the possibilities exist for you and all of those people in your local area and further afield, who you could be helping out of pain.

YOU AND YOUR BUSINESS

Before we wade into marketing and how it works, we'll share a few more important words about that most neglected component in most practices: you, the owner, who often also serves as the lead clinician.

As we've shared, your business should bring you happiness, fulfilment, and reward. These are crucial to your success, yet so many practice owners feel far from achieving anything resembling this. Also, where in any formal business plan is there a box given over to the creation of happiness or fulfilment? The simple answer is you won't find one! There never is one. Yet highly credible research projects have shown time and time again that happiness is a significant contributor to the success and longevity of any business enterprise. To succeed in practice, it's imperative that you give some thought to these things, because in order to persevere and move from stuck to success, you must experience happiness, fulfilment, and reward in your practice.

A note about work-life balance: The term *work-life balance* is misleading, for one very simple reason. The two elements *work* and *life* are the same thing. This very moment that you're reading these words is one moment of your life – whether you're sitting on a bus, on a beach in the Caribbean, or on a coffee break at work. Every minute we're alive and breathing is part of our life. Life doesn't stop when you step through the doors of your practice or sit at your computer in your dining room late at night doing your tax return.

Life is now — every minute of every day.

So in relation to your business, why the heck would you want it to be any less of a rewarding, fun, happy, exciting or enriching experience than snorkelling the Great Barrier reef, becoming a parent, buying your first car, or volunteering in Africa? We certainly don't want that for you. You owe it to yourself to craft a business that brings you happiness, fulfilment, and reward. And because it's your business, you can absolutely do that. You can make the decisions that make your vision a reality.

What the heck has all of this got to do with marketing? It's simple. The things that contribute to happiness in your practice, providing fulfilment and reward, are:

- What you do with your time (clinical services, admin, supporting people, nurturing relationships, etc.)
- Who you spend your time with (your patients, team, suppliers, and community)
- Where you work (the building, your clinic, and the external environment)
- What rewards you receive (emotional and financial)
- How you run the business (your underpinning values, ethics, and processes)
- When you work (full-time, part-time, weekdays, evenings, or weekends).

Hopefully as we go through this floor and peel back the layers of marketing, you'll see how much it relates to each of these factors contributing to your happiness at work. Marketing, and what you do with it, gives you the power to shape your practice. The services you offer, the team, the patients you surround yourself with, the environment you work in, what profit you make, and rewards you receive as well as the hours and when you work – all of these are controlled by your marketing. As the business owner, you're free to decide what all of these things look like for you. Using your marketing wisely, you can bring your vision alive.

Now do you see the connection between marketing and living your most fantastic life? There's also an added bonus to building your business in this very intentional way. Promoting your practice, encouraging others to spread the word, and digging deep when the going gets tough will be much easier if you love what you do. If you really care about the business you're building, then promoting and selling your services will be much easier. The tough days won't be so tough. And your patients will see your passion and become much more likely to share your enthusiasm and spread the word.

If you don't care about the components that make your business amazing, why should anyone else? We want to encourage you to use marketing to help build something you really love.

THE FOUR ESSENTIAL INGREDIENTS FOR EFFECTIVE MARKETING

Before you even begin to think about advertising, Facebook posts, or referral systems, you need to understand and commit to the following four elements. These are what it will take to become great at marketing.

First, you need *clarity*:

- Clarity around *what you want to build your practice into* (see Floor 1)
- Clarity around *what it is you want to be famous for locally*
- Clarity around *who you're serving*

These components alone can skyrocket the effectiveness of your marketing. And they're missing from 90 percent of healthcare practices we see, both in our coaching work and by observing practices around us.

Second, you need *discipline*. You need to turn up every week and dedicate time to learning marketing as well as doing marketing. We encourage you to actually schedule time every week as *marketing time* – time to learn, and time to implement. Marketing takes time – so guess what? You must make time. This need won't go away! Being disciplined about this will make a huge difference.

Third, you need *consistency*. You need to be consistent with your:

- Messaging
- Branding
- Target audience
- Marketing activity.

Marketing isn't something you can afford to faff about with. You reap what you sow. Going at this in a half-hearted way won't bring you the rewards you're hoping for. You either need to get consistent with your marketing, or find someone you can pay to be consistent on your behalf. Either way, consistency is crucial.

Fourth, you need *honesty*. You will need to be brutally honest with yourself and the people around you. Delivering a brilliant experience that your patients love from start to finish and happily pay for requires some honest answers to tough questions.

You won't come out on top of your local market if you pretend to yourself that your website is brilliant, your booking system is slick, your clinic environment is beautiful, and your clinical skills really deliver the goods for your patients, if that's all a bag of lies. Clarity, discipline, consistency, and honesty are required to smash your marketing out of the park and build a thriving practice that you love.

"Enter only those who are not afraid to try."
(Chinese proverb)

WHAT EXACTLY IS MARKETING?

Let's start by getting really clear on what we're talking about when we discuss marketing. In a nutshell, marketing is made up of 7 Ps:

- **Product** – the service combined with any physical product you're selling
- **Pricing** – how and what you charge
- **Place** – where you do business both on and offline
- **People** – everyone involved in delivering and receiving your services
- **Processes** – business systems your patients are part of
- **Promotion** – how you raise local awareness of your practice and what you do
- **Proof** – evidence that you can do what you say you can

Many practitioners believe that marketing is just the stuff you do when you're promoting your practice, when in reality any time you're working on developing any of these 7 Ps, you're working on your marketing. Marketing, as an endeavour, includes knowledge and skills required to:

- Understand your dream patients and what their pain points are
- Reach out and connect with them using words and images that resonate, before they've even met you
- Make a good stab at building a real human relationship with these total strangers, often through the impersonal medium of the Internet
- Persuade them that you're the practitioner who understands them, really cares about them, and has the skills to help them resolve their pain

- Develop and price a service or patient experience that your dream patients will feel real value from, becoming happy to tell other people how amazing you are and how much you helped them

Hopefully you can now see how big a subject – with a broad set of skills – marketing actually is. We don't tell you this to make you even more concerned about the uphill task ahead of you, but to help you cut yourself some slack. You're a clinician, not a marketer, so you're starting from ground zero. That position is normal and fine – and something we can work with.

WHY YOU NEED MARKETING

In our time working with healthcare practitioners, we've come across some practices that have maxed out on their patient bookings, so they stopped doing any kind of promotional marketing and started a wait-list for new patients. This will never work as a business strategy.

First, people looking for a healthcare practitioner are generally looking for prompt treatment. So putting them on a waitlist won't work, unless they get offered a cancellation within a day or so. Pretty soon, they will be looking elsewhere for their treatment.

Second, even if your books are full now, if you stop all kinds of marketing – including encouraging existing patients to make referrals – your patient numbers will drop. This is because:

- Hopefully some of your existing patients will be cured and no longer need your services.
- Not to put too fine a point on it, but patients will die.
- Some patients will move away.
- Others will, despite your best efforts, take their business elsewhere.

Your patient numbers will naturally decline because of those four reasons. So you must maintain some marketing activity to keep your practice topped up, even if the numbers you need are relatively small.

You also must maintain some internal marketing – nurturing relationships with your existing patients – because even if you think they will be loyal, some can still be persuaded to go elsewhere by external factors. They may receive great marketing by a competitor or a personal recommendation from a trusted friend.

Please also bear in mind that replacing patients that leave or stop rebooking will merely keep you standing still. If your vision is to expand and grow your practice and help more patients, then you will need a great marketing strategy.

If you feel you have no need for marketing, we want to assure you that you still require both external and internal marketing, even when things are going swimmingly.

HOW MARKETING WORKS

Marketing is a long game.

We're going to say that again to make sure it has sunk in:

Marketing is a long game!

Yes, you can push out adverts and run campaigns to attract a wave of new patients in a short period of time. But to grow a sustainable business with a depth of loyal patients takes time. To create a steady flow of these good-quality patients into your practice, sleazy-cheesy or quick-win tactics won't serve you in the long run. Marketing is all about building relationships, and that takes time and authenticity. There's a phrase that you may have heard of already:

"People buy from people they know, like, and trust."

This concept is especially true in healthcare, where we can physically touch our patients, ask them intimate questions, or deal with sensitive or emotional issues. Patients buying these kinds of services want to buy from people who they feel they can trust with their health, bodies, and often personal information. "Ah but..." we hear you say, "a large number of patients seek help for acute problems over very short periods of time, so how on earth can it be a long game?"

Well, it works in two ways. First, you may have built up a local reputation to the extent that someone could find you through a referral. If they can be on the phone to you within ten minutes of receiving the recommendation – awesome. But think about it, how long has it taken you to build that local reputation, to develop your relationship with the person making the referral? Far longer than ten minutes.

Second, if someone has an acute problem but doesn't know anyone they can turn to for a recommendation, what do they do? Simple – they jump online looking for a quick solution. They search, and your Google My Business profile pops up. They scan that profile, see some great reviews from existing patients, and use the link to head over to your website. Once there, they watch your introductory video, scan your about page, read a couple of blog posts that relate to the acute problem they have, and follow a link to your social media profile – where they learn about your involvement in a local charity that's close to their heart, that you're a dog owner too, and that you look like you run a professional but fun practice. They're convinced you're the person to help them. They hop back to your website and click the link to book you online.

It's all done within ten minutes. *But* all of the content that they've just consumed to help inform their decision has taken months, if not years, for you to produce and disseminate into the world. So we say it again: Be prepared. Marketing is a long game!

THE PATIENT MARKETING CYCLE

You need to take almost every new patient through a specific cycle to help create and nurture your relationship with them. It looks like this.

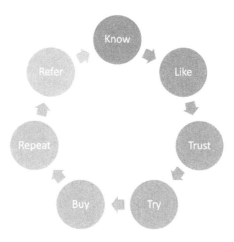

Your job is to understand what each phase of the cycle is – and to make sure you have marketing activity in place that helps move people from one phase to the next. At each phase of the cycle, potential patients will have questions, barriers, and friction that stops them from becoming a patient. Your marketing must overcome those barriers and reduce any friction or concerns.

First things first, *your marketing must work to ensure people in your local area know you exist. You must be visible online and offline. This is where steps like claiming and using your Google* My Business profile, optimising your website for local search, making your social media profiles focused locally, and updating your online directory listings will all help you online. Offline, make sure that the exterior of your premises is spreading the word, you're out and about at local events and clubs, and you're staying connected with all of your local potential referrers on a regular basis.

Second, you must *work at helping people decide if they like you.* We've already identified that people buy from people. So, your marketing must help people make human connections with you and your team by being authentic and not corporate. You will want to show yourself and your team as people, not as clinicians. Don't shy away from showing yourselves as dog owners, keen cyclists, parents, or artists – anything that will help you connect with your dream patients on a personal level. Show your personalities as well as hobbies, skills, and interests. The best places to do this are your website about page, your social media profiles and posts, and of course at local, face-to-face events.

Third, you must *build trust.* This is where your clinical skills, experience, and impact come in. You want to show people the transformations you produce for your patients. Let them see you actually treating patients, hands-on. Share articles you've written or teaching videos you've made. Don't major on your qualifications but on *how you help* – and *how good you are at what you d*o. Make people care about you, by showing that you care about others first.

Fourth, you must *enable people to try out your skills and knowledge before they book you.* Again, this can happen through tools like educational videos, downloadable exercise sheets, or tick lists to help with buying new equipment – anything really that they can take away and try for themselves to see if what you're talking about works. Even if they don't implement it, or it doesn't work for them, you will have built some degree of reciprocity, because you've given your expertise for free. This makes it more likely that when they stop trying to self-treat and want to book a professional clinician, they will think of and schedule with you.

Fifth, you must *make buying from you super easy.* Is it obvious what services and products you're selling? If not, clarify on your website, on your leaflets, in your window displays, and throughout your social media profiles exactly what you're selling. Remember that you're selling transformation and solutions to specific pathologies, not specific treatment plans. Is it easy – like, super easy – to book an appointment? Can people book and pay online? Can they pay by credit card? Can they pay for a block of treatment in advance? Tell people what payment methods they can use and what medical insurance companies you work with. Minimise any friction or barrier to buying. All of these features make the buying process simple to understand and execute.

Sixth in the cycle is *repeat.* In healthcare, we must be very mindful of ethical recalls. Is it necessary for your new patient to come back and see you for a repeat appointment? If so, awesome – make rebooking really easy. Include recommending or scheduling a return appointment part of the treatment plan and clinical consultation. It's not the job of support staff or the patients themselves to negotiate a follow-up appointment. It must be part of the treatment plan that you've already agreed with the patient. You're the experienced clinician and the person best placed to judge what will serve the patient. You recommend if and when they should return.

The final phase in the cycle is *refer.* This is where you set up a system, asking existing patients for their referral of family and friends. This can be accompanied by a reward scheme, or a simple thank-you card works just as well.

Asking for referrals needs to be part of your business systems. Again, this is the role of the clinicians in your practice, not support staff. Patients with whom you've established a good relationship are the ones you should be asking. Asking towards the end of the consult gives weight to the request, as it's coming from the trusted clinician. You may say:

- "We'd really like your help if that's possible."
- "We want to develop our practice and find more patients like you who are struggling, so that we can help them"
- "Would you be happy to help us?"

Then give the patient a really clear way to follow through, such as saying:

> *"If you know anyone who you think we could help, please give them this card (on the back of which you write the name of the referring patient) and ask them to bring it with them when they come in. We'll be sure to take great care of them!"*

Use that card to record the referral and send out a thank you letter and/or reward to close the loop.

Hopefully you can see how old-school, sales-based marketing tactics – BOGOF (buy one get one free), sale on now, or limited time offers don't come in until the fifth element of the cycle. Everything up to that point is much softer and all about helping, nurturing, raising awareness, and making human connections.

"We need to stop interrupting what people are interested in and become what people are interested in."
(Craig Davis n.d.)

WHO ARE YOU SERVING?

Jill started her healthcare marketing business working mainly with podiatrists, and a huge number of practitioners in private practice would tell her that their target audience was "anyone in their local area with foot or leg problems." But if that was the case, how could they make their website effective enough to connect with a seventy-eight-year-old arthritic bowls player, a young mum with toddler trouble, an injured teenage athlete, and a twenty-seven-year-old stroke patient? The answer is simple: They can't. It's not possible.

A potential patient lands on your website looking for confirmation that they're in the right place. Yet there's no way you can build a website that will make every one of those different patient groups feel they're indeed in the right place. There's also no way you can create a leaflet, social media profile, radio advertisement, or video that will resonate with everyone. Another common marketing phrase is:

"If you're marketing to everyone, you're marketing to no-one."

In attempting to market to everyone, you're wasting your time, money, and energy. You need to get focussed. We know this sounds scary, but please bear with us.

Being able to create effective marketing isn't the only reason you must get specific. There are other reasons why you don't want to attract absolutely everyone to your practice. As we've discussed in previous floors, you don't want more of the patients who:

- Have pathologies you're not good at treating
- Always turn up late for their appointments
- You don't enjoy spending time with
- Don't comply with their self-care plans
- Don't attend their appointments
- Grumble about paying
- Have problems that you don't have the capacity to treat
- Don't like the way you do a certain thing
- Want appointments in an evening, if you don't work evenings
- Are mood-hoovers and sap your will to live.

You don't want any more of these people in your practice. Agreed?

Your objective, instead, is to build a practice that makes you happy and delivers a service that your patients love. You cannot be all things to all people. You cannot please everyone. So you must get specific about who your dream patients are. Who are the people you love to serve? For many practitioners, this is very challenging, because they fear excluding anyone, turning good money away, or not serving everyone in their local community. But the truth is, as much as some patients aren't for you, you wouldn't have some patients' best interests at heart if you took them into your practice.

It's in your best interest and the patient's best interest to be selective about who you attract.

LET'S GET PERSONAL

As we've suggested earlier, you need to spend time clearly identifying who your dream patient is. Notice the singular! One person. You must be able to describe them in great detail and know them intimately. That way, you can build a patient experience which they will really value. And you can market that experience directly to the right people, who will be very happy to book that all-important first appointment and pay for the service and value they receive.

EXERCISE
Getting to Know Your Dream Patient(s)

Just to be very clear, you're looking to build a detailed picture, an avatar, of one patient only. To help you get to know your dream patient(s), and to understand them and communicate better with them, work through the following six steps to build your own dream patient avatar. This may feel trivial, you may even feel resistant to doing this, but it's SOOOOO important!

STEP 1: Give Your Dream Patient(s) a Home – by setting up a folder on your computer called My Dream Patient/s.

STEP 2: Document the Demographic and Ethnographic Details of Your Dream Patient(s) – by making a list of their:
- Age/gender
- Appearance
- Occupation and income
- Family life
- Home and car
- Values and beliefs
- Entertainment and reading
- Online search habits
- YouTube watching habits
- Blog reading
- Personal development interests
- Hobbies
- Treats
- Role models
- A fan of…
- Shopping habits – products and brands
- Travel – dream holidays
- Friendships
- Add any other differentiating factors you can think of

Now you should be able to picture this person or these people clearly in your head.

STEP 3: Write a Detailed Description of Them and Their Life – by using the information you've given yourself in STEP 2, joining all the dots together in a descriptive narrative. Save it to your dream patient folder.

STEP 4: Give Them a Name – Yes really, give them a name. Remember you need to really "know" this person. You must be able to bring them to mind every time you create any marketing activity or material. Giving them a name will turn them into a real person.

STEP 5: Create a Dream Patient Board – If you're a Pinterest user, then set up a private dream patient board. Collect images to represent your dream patient and pin them in your dream patient board inside Pinterest. If you're not a Pinterest user, do the same thing, but save the images into a dream patient Word document or PowerPoint presentation. As many images are protected by copyright, just make sure you keep any Word document or PowerPoint presentation private and never share them online or publicly. This step will help you truly visualize your dream patient.

STEP 6: Write a Narrative by Your Dream Patient – by considering the answers your dream patient would give to the following questions:
- What emotion are you feeling around the health problem you have?
- What internal dialogues are you having about it?
- What are your pain points/concerns/objections to paying for it to be resolved?
- What story are you telling yourself about the problem and solution?
- What might happen if the situation gets worse?
- What words and phrases are you using?
- What dream solution would you be willing to pay for?
- What would the dream solution look like as the story unfolds?
- What would you be able to do/achieve if this came true?

Next, write their responses as a narrative about the problem they're having, which you as a practitioner could help them with. Write it as the patient's response, in the first person, and save it into your dream patient folder.

That's it! You're now much closer to knowing and understanding your dream patient.

USING YOUR DREAM PATIENT RESOURCE

Hopefully this process has helped you see and understand your dream patient or patients a lot more clearly. Referring to your dream patient folder will help you:

- Write words that appeal to them
- Create an environment they love
- Develop a service they will want to return to time and time again, telling their friends about it.

You should use your dream patient folder as a resource when writing content for your website, conducting marketing campaigns, and developing your services. Keep listening to your patients, and keep your dream patient documents topped up with new words and ideas. This process of defining and refining your message to your dream patient should never be "finished."

DON'T PANIC – THE RIPPLE EFFECT TO THE RESCUE

The thought of narrowing down the focus to one group of patients causes many practitioners to get agitated and stressed. But worry not, getting focussed will improve both the quality and number of new patients attracted to your practice.

When you start focusing on one specific patient, developing a service for them, and marketing specifically to them, you often experience the opposite of what you're possibly fearing. Your marketing will increasingly attract more of these patients, because you know their exact pain points and concerns and can talk directly to them in your material. Then, because your service is tailored to them, they will have such a positive experience that they'll sing your praises from the rooftops. This will help you attract new patients in the form of family and friends. These patients are a lot like your existing patients, because your marketing will resonate with them too. With us so far? Finally you'll also attract the people who live or work just round the corner, because you're the most convenient solution to their problem.

Can you now see how focusing on one dream patient will help you fill your practice with many more of those dream patients, but also not to the total exclusion of everyone else?

OK, hopefully you're still with us. By now you've learnt more about how marketing works than a vast majority of other local practitioners ever will.

WHAT ARE YOU ACTUALLY SELLING?

Next, we want to talk about what you're actually selling. You must be clear on this if you're going to be successful at marketing it. Many practices we work with fall into three trains of thought here:

- Practices who are focused on filling their clinic – they're selling appointments.
- Practices who are focused on giving of themselves in the service of others – they're usually really poor at selling anything (and often not making much money).
- Practices who are focused on the clinical treatment – they're selling a cure for their patients.

In reality, what every single practice is actually selling, no matter what their area of clinical expertise, is a *patient experience* – with a *transformation* thrown in for good measure. Jill saw a great quote, which goes something like:

"You're not running a business; you're creating a destination!"

The idea being that scruffy, cold, dated, and dirty premises with manual booking systems and slow communications aren't good enough. You must think like a tourist destination and deliver an experience – not just a visit. We live in a consumerist society. No matter how altruistic you feel about providing health and well-being for your patients, they're looking for a great experience. The bar of expectation is constantly being raised, and the practices that are going to survive and thrive are those that embrace the notion of delivering a patient experience. They set about making their practice the bees' knees.

The patient's experience starts with their very first contact with you – whether that's your website, someone answering the phone, a presentation you gave, a social media post, your window display, or an article you wrote in a specialist journal. These are all touchpoints, and all the touchpoints someone has with your practice make up their patient experience. Consider your:

- Premises
- Communication
- New patient pack
- Facilities
- Clinical skills
- Website
- Systems
- Team
- Welcome
- Social media
- Follow-up

We could go on, but we're sure you get the picture. Every single element of the experience can add or detract from a patient's opinion of your practice.

Now we want to make something very clear at this point. The patient experience that you craft for your patients doesn't need to be world-beating. You don't need to be gold-plating everything and serving caviar snacks. But the experience does need to be better than that of most other practices in your local area – something that your dream patients really connect with, which makes you proud.

DELIVERING WOW!

Consumers are becoming more and more discerning. The level and quality of the customer engagement bar has been raised. Mediocre is no longer good enough. Your patients want:

- Value for money
- To feel special
- To feel valued
- To have their time respected
- To have their problem resolved
- To have their life transformed.

The patient experience that you structure must intentionally address each one of those elements, but it also needs to be something that makes you proud and happy. It's important that you like what you create: First, because that will make you feel great, which is very important. Second, it will give you the confidence to price it appopriately and not under-charge. And third, it will drive your desire to market it well, so that more and more patients can experience and benefit from it.

In your marketing, you'll discuss the service that you deliver and the outcomes received. Obviously (but I'm going to say it anyway), you need to be realistic and honest about what you can achieve in terms of clinical outcomes. You also need to be sure that you can deliver 100 percent of what you promise in terms of the service, appointment availability, facilities, and aftercare.

To deliver a **WOW**, you must raise the bar on patients' expectations and then deliver at that level or higher. You only get one opportunity to live up to expectations. The first few days and weeks comprise a very important part of the patient experience – like the police's "golden hour" to find someone when they go missing.

Once you know exactly who your dream patient is, you can structure a patient experience that they will love, benefit from, and be very happy to pay for. As long as you raise the bar and then consistently deliver what you say you will to your dream patients, your practice will thrive.

BARGAIN HUNTERS

Just a quick word about price-sensitive bargain hunters. People who buy a product or service based solely on price will never be loyal. They will forever shop around for the cheapest deal. You don't want those people in your practice. So never make your pricing part of your patient experience planning, and never aim to compete on price.

Dear Jonathan – What Do You Include in Your Patient Experience?

For me, the patient experience begins before they've even heard of me or my clinic. It begins with helping my profession of podiatry to have a positive image in the eyes of the public, who are of course my prospective patients. I don't want them to stereotype me having read or heard about bad experiences with colleagues elsewhere – either NHS or private. I want the public to think that when they have a foot-related problem, their first port of call should be to see a podiatrist as the specialist who can assess, diagnose, treat, and refer within the foot health profession or beyond it. So I work hard to improve the image of podiatry, as that will have multiple benefits, including to my own practice.

I also try to give to anyone who may be interested in receiving. Sharing my time or knowledge for the benefit of others helps them make an emotional connection with me and/or my business. For instance, my clinic website has lots of free information about feet and their related problems. I make myself available to help with any enquiries via email, telephone, or messaging, although my reception staff are trained to work the vast majority of those communication channels. My staff always have a friendly, helpful, efficient approach, so that patients can feel that they know, like, and trust my clinic to help them with whatever problem they have. This applies to any contact we have with our customers – prospective, new, or existing.

The ambience of my clinic is welcoming and helpful, with a warm, homely reception area, and a smiling staff member to help anyone entering. The clinic room is light, refreshing, and ergonomically laid-out for the benefit of both the patient and any clinician. In our dealings with the public, we always try to take a "YES" approach whenever we can, rather than saying "NO." This takes some effort, but we reap the rewards.

Finally, we value any feedback we receive, so that we can continually improve our patient experience. In so doing, we have happy patients, which is good for business.

NOW YOU'VE GOT TO SELL

The current trend is for *pull marketing* – in which you create a lot of useful content so that people can get to know you, like you, and trust you before buying. This means that a large proportion of your marketing material won't be focused on selling. But at some point, you must put your products or services in front of people, so they know what you're selling.

In healthcare, because we've all grown up going to the doctor's or the dentist's office, we generally understand the model that as patients, we're buying into an appointment. But in order to confirm in people's minds that they're making the right buying decision, you generally need to be a bit more specific when you compose your sales-based marketing material.

There's a way to do it, and a way not to do it. In marketing, there's an adage:

"Sell them what they want; give them what they need."

What this means is that in your marketing, you will talk about the things that your patients want as a result of coming to see you (the transformation). This may include:

- Reduced pain – physical or emotional
- Improved function
- Improved quality of life
- Achievement of a desired goal.

Then when they come to see you, what you actually give them is a certain treatment plan that leads to the transformation. A great example of this can be seen in the information technology (IT) industry. Hosting companies (the people who give your website an online home) are selling security, peace of mind, no hassle, time-saving, and automated systems. What they actually provide are servers, wires, and software. If they tried selling just the latter, they'd struggle to make many sales.

Do you see the difference? Let's explore how this plays out in a healthcare setting. Sell them what they want. Craft your promotional marketing around the transformation you deliver. You're taking people from pain, frustration, embarrassment, isolation, worry, or resignation to relief, pride, improved quality of life, a return to what they love, joy, excitement, ease of mind, and even winning that race.

Give them what they need. Use clinical treatments aligned to their problem and desired outcome. What you specifically do with your patients when they come to see you isn't as important to most patients as the results certain treatments can provide. Your sales-based marketing therefore shouldn't focus as much on these services or specific treatments. Most patients won't know what treatment they need. They know what problem they have and what a great outcome would look like, but they don't know how to get that result.

Also, talking about the treatment process is very unemotional, and many purchasing decisions are fuelled by emotion. So, if your sales-based marketing is focussed on the transformation you can provide for certain problems, that will connect on a much more emotional level than talking about actual clinical services that you provide.

This information can also help you structure your website. If you understand that people are aware of their problem and not the solution, you can create pages, sections, and blog posts that talk specifically about problems like "knee pain" or "shoulder pain," rather than talking about ultrasound therapy or deep tissue massage. The latter may mean nothing to your patients, so they won't relate to your online content.

STRUCTURING YOUR PROMOTIONAL MARKETING

Let's start putting these pieces together and helping you get a plan in place. First, get clear on your messaging. Your promotional marketing for your practice must be very focused on helping you becoming famous locally for the thing you do. This is not the *Hello* magazine kind of glossy fame, but rather an approach that makes you the place everyone recommends when a specific problem comes into the conversation. Ask yourself, what conversation do you want to own? If people in your area are talking about shoulder pain, failing eyesight, falling athletic performance, or persistent verrucae, and that's the thing you help people with, you want to dominate that conversation locally. Your promotional marketing planning starts with deciding what you want to be famous for.

To demonstrate this perfectly, here is a real-life example from the editor of this book, to show how marketing to young athletes is working well:

> *"My seventeen-year-old daughter was a competitive run-ner with major injuries three years ago. Four surgeries later, she's reached the end of what the regular medics can do. Today she researched and found a clinic that does treatments like dry needling, etc. She went and came home RAVING about it. "Mom, it was filled with athletes my age, all of whom have had injuries and exhausted the traditional PT route. They offer a whole bunch of services besides dry needling. I'm so excited!" She was hooked by the experience. Now she wants them to handle whatev-er other treatments they might recommend, because she loved the experience. She also got from their website that they catered to young athletes. They're doing a great job of marketing to their niche. I'm paying a lot more for this service than her normal PT, but it's totally worth it, even if just to see the hope she has again that she will get back to running and health soon."*

Once you've decided what you want to be famous for, you need to craft that into words – a short paragraph that you and your team can repeat over and over again. This is your value statement. It's the answer to the question, "So what do you do?"

Your value statement could go something like this:
I'm a specialist shoulder osteopath – I help busy working parents overcome the frustration and limitations of

shoulder pain, so that they can live the active life they want while enjoying time with their children.

Or:

We're a podiatry centre of excellence – We help the athletes and active people of York overcome foot and leg injuries to regain and retain their mobility, so that they can stay active, healthy, and competitive.

Or:

We're a team of multidisciplinary health professionals, helping women under fifty struggling with the physical and emotional effects of early menopause to beat their symptoms, so that they can love themselves and their lives.

OK, now it's your turn.

EXERCISE
Writing Your Value Statement

STEP 1: Write down a few key words on a piece of paper that describe who your dream patients are.

STEP 2: Write as many words as you can onto pieces of paper that describe the pain, both physical and emotional, that your patients are feeling before they see you.

STEP 3: Next, write down words that describe how they're feeling after they've been treated by you – including words that detail the transformation you provide in their lives.

STEP 4: Then cut all those words up, so that each word is on one piece of paper.

STEP 5: Now start playing with those words and add in a few new ones, so that you can put together a value statement that makes the following statements clear to you and attractive to your dream patients:

I'm/We're_____.

I/We help_____ to overcome/recover from_____

so that they can_____.

Once you have your value statement sorted, you then need to dissect it down into a short, snappy *strap line*. This is one sentence that summarises exactly what you do or supports your brand. Look at Nike's and McDonald's with "Just do it" and "I'm lovin' it!" Whilst their slogan doesn't describe what they do (they have enough brand recognition), it summarises a feeling that they want to be connected with. They've stuck to one strapline for years. Similarly, repetition of a single clear message will get you recognised locally for the thing you do. So you must be able to articulate exactly what that is – as succinctly as possible. As an example, here's an expansion on a value statement we already shared:

> **Value Statement:** *We're a team of multidisciplinary health professionals, helping women under fifty fighting the physical and emotional effects of early menopause to beat their symptoms, so that they can love themselves and their lives.*
> **Strap Line:** *Fighting menopause – love yourself and your life*

The final piece of the puzzle is a hashtag that conveys your strapline, or an even more succinct summary of it. Using the same example:

> **Hashtag:** *#figtingmenopauselovinglife*

Once you've got all of this figured out, your job is then to use these words to consistently convey your message. Use your value statement on your website, in your advertising, on your social media profiles, and anytime anyone asks you, "What do you do?" Use your strapline on your signage, on your business cards, in social media posts, in your email signature block, and on printed leaflets or flyers. Finally use your hashtag on everything! If you make it something that's not being used at all by anyone else, you can use it as a tool to track social media activity involving your brand too.

Now, it's time to start taking action. Once you're clear on your messaging, you must start working hard to consistently broadcast that message into your local community. That marketing activity needs to be broken down into the following.

- **Internal** – nurture relationships and continue to educate existing patients and encourage referrals. Nurturing takes time and ££, but it's cheaper and easier than searching for new patients.
- **External** – work to attract new patients and referrers to you. Searching for and connecting with individual patients is hard work, so prioritise building connections with potential referrers. You can reach both internal and external networks with:
- **Ongoing marketing** – this is activity marketing both on and offline. Consider presenting at events, e-mail marketing, social media, blog posts, window displays, leaflets, advertising etc.
- **Campaign marketing** – this is very different from ongoing marketing. You use campaigns when you're looking to attract a wave of new patients – if you have a new clinician or a new service, for example. A campaign includes a lot of marketing activity around one key message over a very short period – making a big noise locally.

Creating an annual rolling calendar that lists all of your elements of promotional activity – including internal, external, ongoing, and campaigns, as well as reviews of your pricing, services, processes, and website – will ensure you identify what you're committed to and where the gaps are. Consistency is the key to successful marketing, so create a schedule where you consider the following activities on a regular basis:

- Post twice a week on your Facebook page.
- Do a Facebook live video once a week.
- Post a new blog on your website every other week.
- Review your pricing structure twice a year.
- Email your existing patients once a month.
- Email referrers once a month.
- Run marketing campaigns three times a year.
- Review your website content once a year.
- Run Facebook/Google ads every week etc.

These methods will help you achieve much better results than random, ad hoc tactics. The list of potential methods you can use is huge, and as we said at the start of this floor, we're not here to teach you how to implement each one – or to tell you that you need to engage in all of them. But we do want to provide a bit of guidance to help you think carefully about the internal and external marketing tactics and tools you select, so that you can get the maximum benefit from the minimum effort. You need to consider questions like:

- Where are the eyeballs of your dream patients online?
- Where do your dream patients hang out offline?
- How can you assist your dream patients with simple, self-help information?
- What social media and other marketing skills do you already have within your team?
- How much time can you allocate each week (remembering you must make time) to your promotional marketing?
- How will you measure the effect of your promotional activity?
- What is your annual budget for promotional marketing?
- Who will be responsible for each element of your promotional work?
- How can you automate some of your internal and external promotional marketing?

Finally, don't forget that you need to choose activities that will move people around the different phases of the patient marketing cycle mentioned earlier on this floor, and you also must make sure that you have promotional activity going on every week, so that you start to build a presence and local fame for the thing that you do.

Dear Jonathan – Have You Always Marketed to Your "Dream Patient"?

In short, the answer to this is a definite no. My private podiatry clinic is based in a small market town. I wanted it to be the go-to place for all foot-related problems in the area. As a novice to marketing back when I started, I'd run generic adverts that to me seemed good, but didn't necessarily hit the spot with my intended audience (i.e., my local community).

Yet my limited advertising success didn't stop my clinic from becoming a success, so I just kept on doing what I'd always done. Unfortunately, this filled my clinic with the four types of clients discussed on Floor 4 – the Awesome ones, the Benign ones, the Cost-Conscious ones, and the dreaded Dire ones! This didn't ensure happiness for me at work and led to me firefighting much of the time.

However, in the 1990s, I started to realise that I was doing podiatry differently from my local competitors. I was focusing on curing foot-related problems (rather than providing ongoing palliative care). So I started marketing on the basis of "fixing feet." And my clinic thrived from my shift to that differentiation. It meant that I attracted clients who wanted their feet fixed permanently, if possible. I achieved a lot of satisfaction from doing that for them, and of course they were delighted that I'd transformed their pain points.

This approach didn't mean that I stopped providing regular palliative foot care for those who needed it – I just didn't market my clinic on that basis. As the number of patients requiring the latter increased, I knew it would threaten my happiness at work, which for me came from solving problems. I therefore took on another podiatrist who was happy with providing the palliative care, and I could keep focussing on fixing feet.

The reputation for my services spread through recommendations, and I realised that my ideal clients weren't necessarily based in my immediate locality. So I started marketing further afield – to find more of my dream patients.

I learnt that targeted marketing worked best, and to do that, I needed to understand more about those patients. I began asking them more about themselves personally (having previously been predominantly focused on their presenting problem). This helped me to understand much more about who my ideal patient was. It became clear to me that I had several types of dream patients, and that trying to market to all of them with a single advert just wouldn't reach all of them, or quite possibly any of them.

Today, I focus a lot on my own marketing. I believe that no one will have as much passion for my business and its values as I have, so I want to communicate that passion to my prospective clients. I can employ people to deliver direct patient care and train them how to achieve the clinical outcomes that I do. But the passion I possess about what we can achieve for our prospective patients requires my voice at the helm. Whilst at times I still find myself reverting to my old impersonalised, scattergun marketing approach, the real rewards for my efforts come from me speaking directly through my marketing to one of my ideal patient avatars (images that represent my dream patients). Whenever I do this, I get more engagement, more enquiries, and more new patients – and they're exactly the type that I want to see, because I focused directly on them.

156

ACTION POINTS TO ENSURE YOU HAVE TAKEN ACTION

☐ Be clear what you want to build your practice into, what it is you want to be famous for locally, and who you are serving

☐ Decide to be disciplined, consistent, and honest

☐ Accept that you need marketing

☐ Understand how marketing works

☐ Complete Getting to Know Your Dream Patient(s) exercise

☐ Deliver WOW!

☐ Structure your promotional marketing

☐ Complete Writing Your Value Statement exercise

☐ Create a Patient Referral Network

YOU NOW HAVE TAKEN ACTION √

NOTES

FLOOR 6 – TRANSFORM:

Moving You and Your Business from Where It Is to Where You Want It to Be

- √ Stop the rot and keep on growing.
- √ Recognise the need to take steps.
- √ Focus on goals and don't procrastinate.
- √ Make small changes to gain momentum.
- √ Change yourself.
- √ Step outside your comfort zone.
- √ Take risks and keep learning.

TAKE RISKS AND KEEP LEARNING.

Our early years in life are all about transformation. From newborn to toddler, from child to adult, every stage involves growth and change. The processes we undergo through those years are designed to enable us to cope better with the challenges ahead. For instance, we need larger skulls to house our larger brains; we need bigger muscles to enable locomotion of our growing bodies; and we need our reproductive systems to mature and ensure continuation of the species.

Once we (successfully) reach adulthood, in many ways we stop transforming. Our skulls are large enough, our muscles are big enough, and our reproductive systems are mature enough to do all that they need to do. However, what then happens at varying points in adulthood is that all of those systems start transforming in the opposite direction. Our skulls shrink with old age, our muscles get weaker, and we're no longer able to reproduce. Some of these we can do nothing about, but we can slow down the weakening of our bodies.

Our muscles respond to load, so we exercise them. We take part in sport, go to the gym, focus on looking after ourselves and our health. If we choose not to, then we're more likely to have problems with our bodies, such as injury, deterioration, and illness. Interestingly, our brains are very similar. If we don't exercise them, then the neural connections (like muscle fibres) get weaker or even disappear.

Over time, it becomes more difficult to come back from the rot that has taken place. Eventually, that ends in our demise, and we're laid to rest. So here's an important question:

If you could stop the rot, would you?

WHY TRANSFORM?

At the start of this book, we looked at change. This tends to be a response to external influences, where we modify our actions to achieve results. Transformation is about modifying our core beliefs and long-term behaviours in order to achieve our desired results, and sometimes that transformation occurs in profound ways.

As we transform through our childhood, our bodies become more able to cope with the next development stage. Then we can transform again and again and again. We see adulthood as the pinnacle of all that, and our bodies generally stop growing and developing. That is, unless we're focused on continued transformation – for example, to become a professional sportsperson. In that case, we train our bodies to be better, stronger, faster. We do it by exercising the required parts of our body – repeatedly, consistently, and progressively. We nourish our bodies with good nutrition whilst avoiding toxic substances, to build the very best version of ourselves and achieve our desired goals. Those goals may be setting personal bests, beating the competition, or reaching the very top of our sport. Alas, few of us will be professional sportspeople. But we're professional healthcare providers.

Fortunately, our brains are part of our bodies, and they require the same discipline. If we want to reach our full potential, we must train our brains to improve. We must exercise that part repeatedly, consistently, and progressively. We must nourish our brains with good information whilst avoiding toxic influences, so that we can be the very best version of ourselves to achieve our desired goals. Those goals as healthcare providers may be reducing pain for patients, improving their mobility, or helping them achieve their own goals.

Never underestimate the power of positive psychology as advocated by one of the leading researchers in psychology, Martin Seligman (also known as "the father of positive psychology"). Your own author, Jonathan, is testament to this source of power to drive positive transformation.

At age forty-two, Jonathan was offered the opportunity to try out for the Great Britain Masters Dragonboat Racing Team. At the time, he'd been a paddler for his local club for a couple of years, with no real competitive sporting experience in adulthood before that. Once he decided to go for a place on the GB team, he knew he had to focus on the end goal of being selected from many other fitter, stronger, better paddlers. Despite the temptation to believe that he wasn't worthy of the GB team, every day he re-iterated to himself that he could and would achieve his goal. Every day, and often several times a day, he'd do something that would move him a step closer towards success. These involved both physical and brain training activities, which utilised his endorphins to help him perform better. After six months of relentless hard work, dedication, and positive psychology, he raced in the national time trials with the seventh fastest time from all those hoping to get in the team. He only needed to be in the top twenty-four, but by committing to the goal, he achieved higher than he could have expected before he started the journey.

In order for our businesses to succeed, they also require such discipline to reach their full potential. We need to train them to be better. We need to exercise them repeatedly, consistently, and progressively. We need to nourish them whilst avoiding toxicity, so that they can be their best to achieve the desired goals. Those goals may be growth of the business, serving the local community, or providing employment opportunities for others.

To achieve the goals for you and your business, you must do tasks:
- Repeatedly
- Consistently
- Progressively

STOPPING THE ROT?

There's a famous saying from Ray Croc, the McDonalds tycoon: "When you're green, you're growing; when you're ripe, you rot." This simple phrase provides the answer. We just need to keep growing. We must stay green in order to avoid the rot. That applies to us and our businesses. When we start to think we or our businesses are ripe, that's when both are at their most vulnerable. Use of the term "we" therefore applies to both ourselves and our businesses throughout the rest of this floor.

We ripen when we reach our goal(s), sit back on our laurels, settle into our comfort zone, and avoid risks. This applies to all aspects of life, and you may think that this is the purpose and pinnacle of humanness. However, we don't agree with this. We believe that continual growth is what matters. It's growth that leads to innovation, creation, capability, creativity, and success. It's the journey that produces the satisfaction and fulfilment. Every step along the way brings you potential to reap great rewards in so many ways, no matter how large or small the steps are.

Therefore, it's actually quite simple to stop the rot – taking steps that help you grow. Any size of step is better than no step at all. But we must be motivated to do so. That brings us back to the question posed earlier on this floor: if you could stop the rot, would you? Unfortunately, the answer is individual to each and every one of us. That individual choice is why some people smoke, over-eat, under-exercise, take illegal drugs, etc. Many would choose to stop the damaging behaviour, but how many of those would actually take the actions necessary to stop? All too often, excuses are given, extrinsic factors are blamed, and there's a lack of personal responsibility for poor outcomes.

KEEP ON GROWING

If we (and our businesses) just kept growing throughout our lives, then we wouldn't ripen and wouldn't rot. So the easiest way to stop the rot is never to stop. This doesn't mean we don't enjoy the view from where we get to on our journey, but it does mean that we keep on moving, no matter how small the steps are that we take. Those steps are many and varied, and some may even seem to be taking us in the wrong direction. But not taking them is actually more harmful to us, as we can learn from our mistakes to stay on track and achieve our goals.

Continual learning is a key part of the growth process, and it comes with so many benefits. This can include *big learning* or *little learning*, depending on how much you're enjoying the view from your achievements, and the time you allocate to the process. But of course, the more you learn, the more you grow. Some of the benefits of learning include:

- It can enhance the services you provide for your patients.
- It can enable you to be a better manager of staff.
- Your brain chemistry changes, and your learning speed increases.
- It fights boredom, and you become a more interesting person.
- You adapt better to change.
- You could stave off dementia.

It's a shame that the benefits of continued growth aren't formally taught in schools. Instead, so many actually disengage from the learning process early in adulthood, or after a goal has been reached (such as enjoying a good job, getting married, having children). They start to rot, but unfortunately often without actually realising that it's happening, especially in the early stages.

The further along the post-ripe rot process we're, the harder it is to reverse the direction – but it's not impossible. There are steps we can take at any stage to ensure our journey is one of growth and achievement.

Dear Jonathan – How Have You Grown Personally Over the Years?

When I qualified as a chiropodist (now podiatrist) in 1990, I was immediately disheartened by NHS work, as it just wasn't what I was expecting it to be. It put me off my chosen profession, and I nearly left it to explore pastures new.

Fortunately, a colleague then inspired me to enter the field of diabetic feet, and I was hooked. I learnt as much as I could as quickly as I could. I contacted knowledgeable people in this field and learnt from them. I worked hard and put that to good use in the care of my patients, helping them to avoid amputations, for instance, and extend their life expectancy.

I worked in various clinics, learning and developing new skills that enabled me to fix feet (which I didn't feel equipped to do from my initial training), and this became my real clinical passion. I then had the opportunity to work in the newly-emerging field of computerised gait and movement analysis. Once again, I immersed myself in the subject, as I strongly believed the more that I put into it, the more I'd get out of it. Applying this knowledge in a rehabilitation setting was truly transformative, as I was helping people to maximise their quality of life.

This approach to learning about any subject to help solve problems is how I operate in life. I will tackle anything from insole manufacturing to website design, from household electrics (before the changes in legislation in the UK) to plastering a wall, from designing an Access database for my mail-order company to creating animated PowerPoint presentations for my business talks. These skills have been learnt, practised, and improved upon, continuing the process year on year.

Alongside this, I have reached out to others, reflected upon my self-understanding, and refined my own personality traits to help me become a better version of myself. Each day, I try to improve in some way – to grow and transform – not only for my benefit, but also for others around me.

RECOGNISE THE NEED FOR STEPS TO BE TAKEN

We cannot transform if we don't recognise the need to do so. Caterpillars have the advantage of something called *juvenile hormone,* the level of which drops to trigger the process of becoming a pupa, ready for rebirth as a butterfly. This is known as complete metamorphosis.

Unfortunately, humans don't have such a hormone to rely on to trigger transformation, so we just have to draw a line in the sand and say, "I've rotted enough now." If we don't, then the rot will continue, and the transformation will be harder when or if it happens. That recognition often, but not always, comes after some crisis moment in our lives. For instance, divorce can result in complete metamorphosis. The caterpillar stage could be the deteriorating marriage, which eventually results in a hardened shell to get through the divorce process, prior to emergence of a new version of the person after the event. After all, very few survive divorce unchanged. It usually comes down to whether the pain of change is more or less than the pain of remaining.

However, we can proactively choose change even in the absence of pain. An easy way to do this is to ask ourselves, "Am I the best version of myself?" If you can't answer that honestly or clearly, then ask those who are close and respected by you.

We all have our good character traits and those that aren't so good. Understanding how we come across to others can be enlightening, educational, and provide a catalyst to change. Don't forget this can also apply to our jobs ("Am I the best healthcare professional I can be?") and businesses ("Is my business the best it can be?"). It would be rare to answer yes to these questions, if you're honest with yourself. And the no answer can provide motivation to change. It effectively draws the required line in the sand when the question is asked. Then it's up to you if you want to cross that line by following your current trajectory – or turn around and look at the goal(s) you've been moving away from instead of towards.

FOCUS ON GOAL(S)

If we don't understand where we're heading, how can we choose which path has the best chance of getting us there?

Wandering aimlessly around without focus will lead to distraction, uncertainty, procrastination, and indifference. None of these are good for a successful healthcare professional – nor for a successful healthcare business.

We – Jill and Jonathan, the authors – are both keen mountain walkers. We frequently set the goal of reaching the top of a mountain, whether that's 1,000m or 6,000m high. The height doesn't affect the process of achieving the goal. This goal-setting can take place days, weeks, or even months/years before the walk begins, depending on the difficulty of the challenge we face. Once the goal has been set, then intentional action towards it takes place. Without that goal, there's no intent, no focus, and no definite direction for the required preparations. And if weren't prepared properly, then we're more likely to fail.

Having defined goal(s) enables us to keep an eye on our route to achieve those goals, ensure that our trajectory is right, and communicate to others who we may need on the journey or just encounter along the way. Setting a goal is easy – just write down what you want and put it in a prominent place so that you see it regularly to remind you. Sharing that goal with others – so that they expect you to achieve it – can create more motivation, as we often find it harder to let others down than ourselves.

DON'T PROCRASTINATE

Motivation can be difficult. We're so easily distracted by other things, whether through our own personal prioritisation of perceived needs, or through our dopamine-related reward system from environmental stimuli. Basically, this means we tend to seek speedy solutions to problems and/or speedy rewards. When we hit a challenge, if we can't solve it quickly, we'll look for something else easier from which to can get a sense of achievement. This is the basis of procrastination that affects so many of us.

Unfortunately, the more we procrastinate in this manner, the more we want to do it. Neurotransmitters like dopamine – which we get when we achieve any reward – are potentially addictive, so it's a hard cycle to break. We, the authors, know this very well. We set ourselves the goal of writing this book a long time before it got published. We knew all the steps required to get to our goal, but distractions with other things in our lives meant it didn't happen as quickly as we'd originally hoped. We didn't have sufficient motivation to overcome the hurdles that cropped up. Even by encouraging each other along the way, we still struggled. In the end, it came down to deadlines. We broke the final goal down into achievable chunks and put timescales on each other to complete those tasks. This made the process more manageable, and what initially looked daunting and not enjoyable soon became achievable and even pleasurable.

MAKE SMALL CHANGES TO GAIN MOMENTUM

The first step is often seen as the hardest. That may be because it involves some grief for us, as discussed in Floor 2. Often when we're reaching towards a positive goal, we're giving something up – even if it's just comfort, a routine, etc. Going on a diet, we may yearn for more health, but we're giving up sitting on the couch in front of the telly and eating our favourite ice cream. The first step is also difficult because we try to achieve significant change quickly, and we feel that requires us to take a big step in the new direction. However, taking such a large step can lead us to feeling unbalanced, unprepared, and more at risk of falling or failure. So the answer is to take smaller, more manageable and realistic steps.

As Jonathan wrote this, his teenage son had just come in from cleaning the cars outside. This was a job that he had procrastinated about all morning, He got distracted by all the easier, dopamine-stimulating things like computer games, watching YouTube, and eating. All of these he could do whilst still wearing his dressing gown. However, he couldn't really clean the cars in that attire. So the first small step was to encourage him to get dressed. This started the journey of several subsequent steps that enabled the goal to be achieved.

If you want to make a change within yourself or your business, then break the process down into small enough steps that you can take that first one with confidence and commitment.

Once you've committed and built your confidence, the traction you gain will lead you to the next step, and the next, and the next. Soon, you'll realise how far/high you've come in just a few steps. Interestingly, those who haven't been party to those small steps may think that you have some intrinsic special talent or personality trait that enables you to make such big changes, or that you're lucky and without the extrinsic restrictions that they blame for their own lack of progress. But you'll know that this isn't the case. All you did was try to take some steps in the right direction.

CHANGE YOURSELF

It's easier to change ourselves than everyone else, but we wouldn't think that to be true from observations of interactions between people. Indeed, wars have been fought over differences in opinion that could have been avoided if there had been understanding and willingness to change and reach acceptable compromises.

The key to changing ourselves comes from having a flexible outlook, one that responds to learning new things and says, "I can" rather than "I can't," and "I will" instead of "I won't." But that's not always easy. We're frequently susceptible to criticism and worry about what others think of us, so we try to protect ourselves with an imaginary shield or bubble. By keeping that protection mechanism strong, we feel safer from personal attack. The downside is that we're then unable to come out from behind our shield to see things from another person's point of view. Our protection reduces our flexibility but reinforces our stubbornness to change.

Fortunately, we all have our raving fans – people who love us for who we are, what we stand for, and what we do. This applies to us as people and healthcare professionals, and also to our businesses. So believe in yourself, as others believe in you. And embrace positive change for the better, rather than letting negativity and criticism stop you from achieving your transformation. Your raving fans will just love you more because of your positivity.

STEP OUTSIDE YOUR COMFORT ZONE

How often do you hear yourself saying "I wouldn't do that" when presented with something outside your comfort zone? That could be talking on stage, going on a theme park ride, or learning a new skill, for instance. Over time, this approach actually reduces the size of your comfort zone, and unless you step outside of it, then you'll rot until you disappear. The only protection from this is to step outside of your comfort zone on a regular basis. The more you do this, the more confident you'll become in doing it, and your confidence will grow. The more it grows, the easier it becomes to step outside your comfort zone again. It's an effective growth feedback loop.

As mentioned before, the first step can be small. Effectively "get dressed," so that you're in a position to say, "I can try doing that!" (Like Jonathan's son getting into the right clothes – or at least out of the wrong ones – to wash the car!) In essence, this involves just a simple change of words. In reality, it comprises a complete reversal from a negative to positive attitude – from a fixed mindset to growth mindset. Yet all that's required is for us to take some risks.

 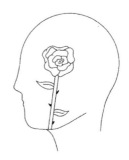

FIXED MINDSET	GROWTH MINDSET
Unchangeable aptitude	Analyses mistakes
Avoids challenges	Accepts challenges
Avoids failure	Ability to learn new things
Gives up easily	Inspired by success of others

TAKE RISKS

Every day, we take risks. When we cross the road, there's the chance of being knocked down. When we fall in love, there's a chance that we'll be rejected. When we start our businesses, there's a chance that they will fail. So we take steps to minimise those risks. We look both ways to make sure it's safe to cross the road. We check that it's safe to open our heart to others by getting to know them first. We do our due diligence to assure us that our business choices are good.

But then we settle. We stop taking risks, because we have some rewards. We convince ourselves that it's safer not to take the risk. We effectively just sit within our ever-decreasing comfort zones. In this process, we forget how good it feels to take risks. We lose the ability to weigh up risk and reward. We forget how to minimise the risks, instead choosing to avoid them.

Whilst having no risk in your life may seem like nirvana, it actually isn't healthy, as we become more fearful and protective of our comfort zone and stability. And external factors beyond our control or foresight can affect or even destroy that nirvana. Far better is to be comfortable with being uncomfortable, as it will make you more resilient to life's challenges. By taking risks as part of a learning process, we then develop and maintain the skills of minimising those risks.

Taking risks is a normal part of business growth. If we aren't taking risks, then we aren't growing.

We should set ourselves a target for risk-taking. This can be based on frequency or significance, but it should involve repetition, reward, and reflection, so that it's beneficial to us and our businesses in as many ways as possible. Those risks can be personal or business-based. Note that sharing the risk can reduce the potential for damage, but it can also reduce the potential reward.

One thing to remember when risk-taking is that the sun will always rise, and the sun will always set. That process of daily renewal has been going on for eons and will continue long after we have departed this world. So, if you take a risk and it doesn't work out well for you, then as long as you have your health, you'll be able to start the next day afresh. It will be up to you how you approach each new day when you wake. That's entirely under your control, as is the decision to take risks or not take them.

Importantly, we need the ability to assess the risks of doing something versus the rewards we may get from it. This is a learned skill developed through personal experience. The more frequently we do this, the more accurate our assessment of risk versus reward will be, and the more chance that we'll end up maximising the rewards whilst minimising the risks.

OUT WITH THE OLD, IN WITH THE NEW

As we discussed on Floor 2, transformation involves letting go. All too often, we hold onto the past – including physical objects and personal emotions or beliefs – even though they don't need to be in our future. Indeed, they can stop us from achieving the future we want for ourselves. So we must let them go. We must declutter our physical and mental space. This can be a painful process for us. However, that pain is only temporary, with a whole world of reward on the other side.

Letting go of our emotions isn't easy. They seem to rule our lives and affect our decisions. There are so many of them as well – just look at how many different emoticons exist for your messaging conversations and social media posts. But it isn't actually the whole emotion that we're trying to let go of. Our emotions are made up of subjective experience, physiological response, and behavioural response. We're really looking to change any or all of those, so that the outcome is better for us.

174

Our physiological response to the subjective experience is where our autonomic, sympathetic, and limbic systems react to the stimulus and create a behavioural response. We can't directly or easily control the physiological response, but we can control the subjective experience. If we can expose ourselves to more positivity and happiness, then our subjective experience will be different than when we're exposed to negativity and sadness. If the input is good, the output should be good. When we can't control the input, we can exert conscious control of our behavioural response to bad input – using meditation and affirmation techniques which require learning and practice.

Now what about letting go of our beliefs, especially the ones that hinder or restrict us? Initially this may seem more difficult than sorting out physical objects. But in fact, it's easier, as once we've let them go, we don't need to take them anywhere. It's crucial to realise that your beliefs are exactly that; they're just yours. Someone else may not share your beliefs. Once you accept that, you can look to see whether your belief is based on fact, or on fear (which is more likely). By introducing a *fact filter* to your thought processes, you'll be surprised at how easy it is to let go of restrictive beliefs. To improve the accuracy and effectiveness of your fact filter, you must learn more.

KEEP LEARNING

Our brains are precious. Without them, we wouldn't exist (in our human form at least). They're made up of many, many neural connections (synapses) – 100 trillion of them! That's more than 1,000 times the number of stars in the Milky Way Galaxy. And they need stimulating to keep working. That stimulation occurs when we "think" – using our minds to actively form connected ideas. Without stimulus, then the synapses disappear over time, and our brains don't function as well as they once did. With stimulus, not only are our synapses maintained, but we can create new ones. In fact, we can even rewire old thought processes to create new, improved ones, as our brains are in fact neuroplastic. This is what happens when we learn.

Learning can come in many ways, shapes, and forms – reading, listening, watching, communicating, etc. We all have our own personal preference for learning, and it really doesn't matter which method we engage in, as long as we do it repeatedly, consistently, and progressively (exactly the same tools discussed earlier). By having a mixture of learning styles, we'll undoubtedly get more stimulus than if we have just one style, but any good stimulus is better than none. But as stated before, be aware of the potential damage of bad stimulus – fake news, misinformation, and untruths aren't good things for our brains to absorb.

Challenging what we have learnt will test and potentially reinforce the neural connections that we make. Discussing acquired information with peers will enable critical appraisal to help ensure our knowledge is sound. That feedback phase is important, so that we can grow and develop to be the best version of ourselves. Note that the critical appraisal process may not be possible from those who love you, such as family and friends. They may not be sufficiently objective enough to challenge you.

Even better than just learning stuff for ourselves is sharing that knowledge with others to help them.

Paying your learning forward creates an upward growth cycle that is beneficial to all. This sharing can be through the written word, audio/video recordings, talks/lectures, and conversation. Interestingly, these are the same techniques that are used for marketing (see Floor 5).

Dear Jonathan – What Has Transformed You and Your Business the Most?

The biggest transformation occurred for me when I stopped trying to be a sheep, following the crowd, running my business the way all other podiatrists seemed to run theirs. Instead, as I've shared, I decided to forge my own path and develop my clinical service the way I wanted to run it for the benefit of my patients. Basically, this meant throwing out the "cut and come again" model of foot care services, and moving to an "I fix feet" model, whereby I would do my best to improve/cure my patients' foot-related problems.

Specifically, I started supplying products to help them take ownership of their foot health needs and to engage them in actively looking after their own feet. This approach was criticised by some colleagues, but I believed in it and the benefits it would bring to my patients, my business, and myself.

Incredibly, my approach started to be emulated by other podiatrists throughout the UK, and so many more practitioners and their patients benefitted from it. This makes me feel proud, as this model has the potential to change the foot health of the nation, which is a noble and worthwhile cause.

Recognising my mindset blocks and releasing myself from them has also helped this transformation. I now do this by looking for these blocks in others, and then seeing if I also have them. If I do, then I develop strategies to help overcome them. Frequently, this involves me just doing the opposite of what a particular mindset block says to prove to myself that it can be done. For instance, if someone says to me, "You can't do something," I immediately think: why not? And generally that's followed with: I can. Initially, I visualize this happening, which is then turned into reality by me actually doing the thing I was told (or I initially told myself) I couldn't do.

I also transformed when exposed to other transformational and inspirational characters – clinical mentors, business mentors, and personal mentors. Their growth/ change messages have rung true with me and helped me and my business to transform.

ACTION POINTS TO ENSURE YOU HAVE TRANSFORMED

☐ Stop rotting and keep growing

☐ Recognise the need for steps to be taken

☐ Focus on goal(s) and don't procrastinate

☐ Make small changes to gain momentum

☐ Change yourself

☐ Step outside your comfort zone

☐ Take risks

☐ Let go of restrictive beliefs

☐ Keep learning

YOU'RE NOW TRANSFORMED √

NOTES

FLOOR 7 – ETERNISE

Perpetuating Your Success and Happiness

√ Be intentional about what you do with your time.

√ Think about longevity.

√ Identify your drivers.

√ Be really clear on your purpose.

√ Innovate and systemise.

√ Foster a positive, healthy culture.

Stephen Covey in his book *The 7 Habits of Highly Effective People* identifies his second habit as "start with the end in mind"(Covey 1989). As this is the last floor of this book, we want to get you thinking about the end of the road for your practice. When will that be? What are your plans for your practice ten, fifty, or a thousand years from now? Will it still be in your family, or will you have sold it within five years for capital gain?

Many practitioners don't ever think this through in advance and find themselves in a mess a few years down the line when the business isn't operating how it needs to in order to sustain itself. These practitioners structure their business around doing what they know how to do as a clinician, but rarely start with any clear or even strong idea about what the end result of all their work will be. To prevent you from being in that situation, let's start to consider perpetuating your success and happiness.

Longevity in business boils down to one thing: continuing to offer products and services that meet the changing demands of your target audience.

Happiness in business boils down to being intentional about what you do with your time — including who you spend it with, what you spend it doing, the environment you spend it in, and how you do the things you do.

Perpetuating your success and fulfilment involves delivering on a combination of these two things. So let's dive deeper into both of these. One thing we need to be clear on from the start is that longevity in business can mean different things to different people. For some, it's about creating an entity that can be passed from generation to generation. For others, it's about doing something long enough to get their children through university or themselves into retirement. For others, it's about growing as big as possible as quickly as possible and selling the business for profit. None of these options are right or wrong. You just have to choose one that feels like the right thing for you.

Commonly called an exit strategy, what are your plans for exiting your business? Are you planning on creating a legacy business that you work in until you retire and can pass it from one generation to the next? Do you want to stop seeing patients at age forty, having set the business to run without you, and draw a salary for the next thirty years? Or are you planning on getting a slick business operation in place, maximising your net profit and therefore business valuation, so you can sell and move on?

The choices you make about your exit strategy will impact other business decisions as you work towards building and developing your practice. You must know what your longevity plan is, so that you can make the right decisions as you progress. So, what does the longevity of your practice look like for you? You need to get really clear on this, so you can set about making it happen.

Dear Jill – What's the Longest-Running Business Ever?

Kongo Gumi was a Japanese Buddhist temple building business run by the Kongo family. Widely quoted as the oldest business in the world, it was founded in 578 (Sone 2013), less than one hundred years after the fall of the Roman Empire. It was a family-owned business right up until its demise in 2006 during the world economic crisis. The business had lasted 1,428 years and had been run by forty generations of the same family.

The last CEO, Masakazu Kongo, attributed their long-lasting success to a consistent focus on its core business, training its craftsmen and women in the art and craft of traditional temple building. But also, over the centuries, they adapted how they worked. They were amongst the first in their industry to use concrete that was textured to look like wood in their constructions, and they were early adopters of computer-aided design technology.

Ironically, two of the factors contributing to their

business demise were: first, the fact that in the 1980s, they diversified into real estate investing – a totally different industry; and second, that they stuck too rigidly to temple construction. A previous foray into coffin manufacturing (still working with wood) had proved very successful. But when society changed after WWII and temple donations that had fuelled their industry dwindled, they didn't look to new ways of using their skills. The temple-building rug was effectively pulled out from under them.

The business is still in existence but is no longer family owned, having been bought by a large construction company in 2006.

Hot on their business longevity heels is Nishiyama Onsen Keiunkan, another Japanese family business – a hotel that has been operating for a mere 1,315 years. Officially recognised by the Guinness Book of World Records as the oldest hotel in the world, they're worth a google if you're looking for some longevity inspiration. (Oldesthotel)

It is worth taking some time to think about what longevity means to you – and for your practice. The longevity vision you have will dictate the business you build, thereby impacting your everyday decisions. The most commonly-cited elements that support the longevity in a business are:

- Clarity of purpose
- Innovative capability
- Effective strategies
- Organisational systems
- Effective resource utilization
- A positive and productive organisational culture – values, expectations, assumptions.

We'll explore each of these elements in turn and give you time to reflect for yourself on where you and your practice sit in relation to these success and longevity factors. But first, in addition to these strategic elements, there's another important factor we want to discuss.

Although not usually part of business courses or traditional business planning, another element we also believe very strongly influences longevity of businesses is *personal contentment.* How you feel in business – in relation to happiness, fulfilment, professional standing, and security – will impact your willingness to do the work to create the longevity you want. Whether you're going for five, thirty, or one thousand years, it will all require hard work.

So let's start working through each element of longevity.

PERSONAL HAPPINESS

We're starting with personal happiness, because as we've suggested throughout this book, above all else we believe that this is the ultimate destination or objective in life. Setting your business up in a way that brings you joy and fulfilment from the outset is one of the most important business success strategies.

One of the most significant elements in the longevity of your practice is you and your ability to be fulfilled by the work you do every day (well, most days!). Without that driver, you'll struggle to sustain your practice in the longer term. It must deliver elements that excite you day in day out, to fulfil you and give you joy. So you must work on intentionally building those elements into your practice.

We looked on Floor 2 at how our emotions (i.e. how we feel) fuel our actions, and in turn how they dictate the results we achieve. We now want to spend some time helping you identify the emotional drivers that are most important to you. If you can build those drivers into the day-to-day operations of your practice, you'll feel far more positive emotions towards your business than if these elements are nowhere to be seen.

Your drivers are the principles, beliefs, and attitudes that guide your behaviour and make you feel positive emotions. When you're not in alignment with your drivers – when you act out of alignment with them – life and business don't work. Things just don't feel right. You procrastinate over doing the things that would move you forward, because you're just not excited by them or the practice you're creating. So, next is an exercise for identifying and optimizing your drivers.

EXERCISE
Identifying Personal Drivers and Building Them into Your Practice

STEP 1: From the following list, pick your top ten drivers in life – no more, no less. These are not the things you think you should pick, but things that really resonate with you and would make you feel positive and excited by your life if you had them. Feel free to add any others that aren't on this list. Put each one you choose on a separate sticky note. We'll then take you through STEP 2 of the process. Note: This isn't a precise science. You can repeat the process a few times to make sure you distil down to your top three drivers. TAKE YOUR TIME. Your best guide is to notice how each driver makes you feel when you read it and imagine it influencing your life. Try to do this for every word on the list, and mark the ones that excite you, to create your initial short list.

Abundance	*Athletics*	*Comfort*
Accomplishment	*Authenticity*	*Commitment*
Achievement	*Authority*	*Community*
Activity	*Autonomy*	*Competition*
Admiration	*Beauty*	*Conformity*
Advancement	*Belonging*	*Connections*
Adventure	*Brotherhood*	*Conservation*
Advocacy	*Caring*	*Consistency*
Affection	*Challenge*	*Control*
Affluence	*Charity*	*Cooperation*
Ambition	*Clarity*	*Creativity*
Art appreciation	*Close friends*	*Credit*
Artistic expression	*Collaboration*	*Culture*

Decisiveness
Discipline
Dominance
Drama
Driven
Duty
Economic security
Education
Employment
Endurance
Energy
Enjoyment
Enterprise
Entertainment
Entrepreneurship
Equality
Equal opportunity
Excitement
Exercise
Experience
Experimentation
Faith
Fame
Family
Flamboyance
Focus
Freedom
Free time
Friendship
Frivolity
Fun
Gentleness
Good income
Goodness
Growth
Happiness
Healing
Health
Helping others
High standards
Holiness
Home
Honesty
Honour
Hope
Humility
Humour
Imagination
Impact
Improving society
Impulse
Income

Independence
Individualism
Industriousness
Influencing others
Inner direction
Inner harmony
Innovation
Integrity
Intellectual
stimulation
Interpersonal relations
Intimacy
Involvement
Joviality
Joy
Kindness
Kinship
Laughter
Leadership
Leisure
Legacy
Life
Literature
Love
Loyalty
Managing
Mastery
Making millions
Maturity
Meditation
Mentoring
Modesty
Money
Morality
Neatness
Nonconformity
Nurturing
Obedience
Order
Outdoor life
Ownership
Patience
Peacefulness
Persistence
Personal development
Philanthropy
Philosophy
Play
Pleasure
Politics
Possessions
Power

Professionalism
Prosperity
Psychic power
Reading
Rebellion
Recognition
Religious beliefs
Reputation
Research
Respect
Respectfulness
Responsibility
Rewards
Riches
Ripples
Satisfaction
Security
Self-expression
Self-reliance
Self-respect
Self-satisfaction
Service
Sincerity
Social connections
Social life
Social recognition
Space
Spirituality
Sports
Stability
Stamina
Strong beliefs
Status
Stimulation
Success
Survival
Taking risks
Teamwork
Technique
Tenacity
Tradition
Tranquillity
Transformation
Transparency
Travel
Trust
Truthfulness
Wealth
Welfare
Well-being
Working with others
Winning

STEP 2: Sit with those ten sticky notes in front of you. We're now going to offer you seven hypothetical situations. You must decide which of the drivers on your sticky notes you would trade for the things we're offering you. This is an all-or-nothing offer. You're guaranteed the thing on the offer, but you can never again have that driver in your life that you're releasing. You're giving it up for life.

▶ What driver would you be prepared to exchange for never having to do any of the tasks you hate doing, domestically or in your business, ever again?
▶ Set that sticky note to one side.
▶ Which driver would you be willing exchange for the smoothest-running, most successful and flourishing practice you can imagine?
▶ Set that sticky note to one side.
▶ What driver would you be willing to exchange for the most loving, supportive, sensual, fun, and happy life partnership?
▶ Set that sticky note to one side.
▶ Now what driver would you exchange for an all-expenses-paid, lifetime ownership of your dream property in your dream residential location?
▶ Set that sticky note to one side.
▶ What driver would you be prepared to exchange for financial freedom and security for the rest of your life?
▶ Set that sticky note to one side.
▶ Which driver would you be willing to exchange for us taking away inner turmoil, personal beliefs, insecurities, lack of confidence, or imposter syndrome, etc. – forces that are holding you back and limiting your life?

Set that sticky note to one side.

▶ Finally, take away the driver that you would be willing to exchange for guaranteed lifelong health for you and your immediate family.

Now you should be left with three post-it notes. We want to suggest that these are likely to be your primary drivers in life.

STEP 3: Review how these drivers are currently built into your business. We want to stress at this point that you're not looking at how your business could facilitate these drivers, but how these drivers are actually built into the fabric of your business. For example, if one of your drivers is adventure, we're not suggesting that you explore the fact that your business pays you well, so you can take exotic holidays. We're asking how you've woven a sense of adventure into how you do business. Are you leading your industry in doing things in new ways? Are you building adventure into your teambuilding activities? Are you being adventurous with the décor in your clinic?

We hope you can see the difference. You must feel these three drivers inside of your business in order to feel alignment and contentment. Once you integrate these key drivers, then you'll become much more likely to feel very positive about your business and enjoy your time in it. And that means you'll also be much more likely to do the hard things.

You must stay inspired and motivated. What does your business need to look and operate like to keep that positive energy alive? You must build those drivers into your business. Building something that you really believe in makes it so much easier to stay energised to work in the long term, and it will make you a happy and powerful advocate of your business too. Loving your practice is a great way to create business longevity.

FLIPPING THOSE CHALLENGES

Many people see the challenges of being in business – the tough days and disgruntled patients – as a negative thing. But we want to see if we can reframe that for you to help you work through those days that don't feel great. Tony Robbins, renowned personal and business development coach, identifies six human needs that, if met, will enable us to feel a sense of contentment (Robbins 2008). He says that to feel contented, we all need:

1. **Certainty** – a deep knowing that you can avoid pain and gain pleasure
2. **Uncertainty/Variety** – the need for the unknown, a change, or new stimuli
3. **Significance** – to feel important, special, or needed
4. **Connection/Love** – a strong closeness or connection with someone or something
5. **Growth** – developing your own capacity, capability, or understanding
6. **Contribution** – a sense of service or focus on helping, giving, and supporting others

First, it would be interesting to see how you view all of these in relation to your practice. How many of these does your practice support you with? All six? Just two?

But the real point we want to make here is that when looking at these six elements, you can see that two of them – uncertainty and growth – can be fuelled by the changing and challenging nature of business. So, when the environment and the way we do business continue to test us and throw up challenges, it's not necessarily a bad thing. If these factors are providing uncertainty and the opportunity for us to grow as people, then they're both positive elements in our businesses. Flip any negative perspective on them, and see them that positive way. That said, they don't need to be huge life-changing challenges.

Simple changes to our environment and our businesses can be enough to perpetuate our success, happiness, and business longevity.

To feel contentment and motivated, we also must be able to see our accomplishments and feel proud of the progress we've made. The difficulty is that often we're so close to everything every day that we can't stand back and see the big picture. Both little and big wins can go unnoticed. To help with this, we want to encourage you to start an achievement jar.

EXERCISE
The Achievement Jar

Acknowledging where you are and the progress you've made is quite easy once you set up this simple process. You just need a jar of some sort, small pieces of paper, and a weekday reminder set on your phone.

At the end of each day, you simply write down on a scrap of paper all the things you achieved. This can be anything from "Today I treated all of the patients in the diary" or "Today I fed myself and my family three meals" to "Today we launched our new website" or "Today we smashed our quarterly financial goal" and anything in between. You achieve a lot most days; it's just that most of it goes unrecognised as an achievement. Not anymore!

Write down what you achieved each day, tiny or huge, and pop the piece of paper into your jar. Keeping a piece of paper handy during the day can encourage you to jot down as you achieve each thing. But you can wait until the end of the day when your reminder goes off – it's up to you. Then, decide how often you need a motivation boost:

► Once a month?
► Once a quarter?
► Once a year?

You decide. Set another reminder alarm on your phone. On the allocated day, empty out your jar and read all the things you've achieved. You'll be amazed at how much you've achieved – and also how much you've forgotten you actually got done. Then simply rinse and repeat this exercise to get ongoing appreciation and motivation from just how far you've come and what you've achieved.

Hopefully this section has given you some ideas about how you can proactively work on your personal contentment, so that you're in the best place to maintain momentum and ensure the longevity of your practice.

CLARITY OF PURPOSE

This is a biggie! To build a sustainable business, you must be really clear on your purpose.

1. What is the core reason for doing what you do at an emotional level?
2. Emotionally, why are you in business?
3. Who do you help, and how do you help those people?

Can you easily and quickly answer these questions? If not, you have some work to do to gain clarity on your purpose (we'll come to that in a minute).

Your purpose should be driving your business decisions every day. If you (as the business owner or manager) can't quickly and simply explain what you do and why you do it, how will you ever explain it to others – including those in your team – so that they can understand and help you get there? Having clarity around your purpose will make you a better leader and enable you to get all of your team members on the same page more easily, with everyone rowing in the same direction.

Much like personal happiness, *clarity of purpose* is another thing you won't find a box for in most standard business plans. This is a big shame, because if there were a box for it, maybe more practice owners would spend serious time defining their *why*. Once you identify and understand your purpose, it's so much easier to motivate yourself and your team on the days when the going gets tough.

We talked about your vision in great detail on Floor 1, and we talked about your why (aka your purpose) on Floor 3 when we discussed creating happiness. Now we want to close the loop by discussing your mission. To help you differentiate your purpose from your vision and your mission, consider the following:

- Your *purpose* is why your business exists – the impact you want to have in the world or the change you want to make.
- Your *vision* is the worldview you will be helping to create by being successful in your purpose. How will being successful in your purpose impact the world around you?
- Your *mission* is what you're going to do to achieve your purpose – that is, the day-to-day work.

To help you see this in action, here is an example from Jill's business, Practice Momentum – a business that on the surface provides marketing training to health professionals in business.

Here at Practice Momentum…
Our purpose (why we're doing this) is to gain huge satisfaction from empowering thousands of people around the world to find and create more joy in their lives by helping others back to health.

Our vision (what this will look like) is that more practitioners and patients in local communities will be intentional about feeling happy, contented, abundant, and healthy.

Our mission (how we'll do this) is to:

- *Create a thriving community of health professionals by caring and providing world-class coaching, education, and support services.*

- *Help health professionals build happy, thriving practices through personal development and marketing education.*
- *Help more people find life-changing healthcare by ensuring our members and clients are more visible.*
- *Create a remote but close-knit expert team inside Practice Momentum that feels supported and rewarded by using great communication, efficient systems, listening, and support learning.*
- *Give poor and vulnerable people a helping hand through time, monetary, and equipment donations to health-related charities.*

Hopefully this helps you see how your purpose can have real emotion attached to it. Your purpose has nothing to do with making money or progressing professionally, but those things will naturally fall out of pursuing your purpose.

Also, we hope you can see how your vision and your mission cascade down from this clear purpose – and how they will drive your decision-making. Having this clarity of purpose will help you make faster and better decisions in your business and guide the actions you take because of those decisions. Better decisions and clear actions will lead to a stronger business, potentially with more longevity.

Having this clarity of purpose will also make you a better leader, who is more able to inspire and motivate the people around you. An important note here is that if you are part of a team and not a lone practitioner, you'll need to make sure your purpose is collective, and not personal. Otherwise getting people to buy into it will be hard. Having clarity of purpose will also help you plan and set goals and targets. Those could seem meaningless – but with a clear purpose behind them, they will move your practice forward on a trajectory that is very clear and more likely to be successful. Your purpose becomes a great filter through which to pass your decision-making questions. When it comes to taking big or small business decisions, you can ask yourself:

- *Will this move us towards our purpose?*
- *Will this support our vision?*
- *Where does this fit into our mission?*

Clarity of purpose will give you real focus, and it doesn't matter if it changes along the way as you and your practice grow. The important thing is that you always have one. It's like your north star guiding your decision-making and actions, creating a strong business with great longevity potential.

"There's one quality which one must possess to win, and that is definiteness of purpose, the knowledge of what one wants, and a burning desire to possess it."
(Napoleon Hill n.d.)

Your clarity of purpose is unlikely to arrive in a blinding flash, and that's fine. Don't beat yourself up if it takes time. Go with the flow and work your way towards something that feels great, rather than plumping for something that comes as a blinding flash at 3:00 p.m. whilst sitting in your car in the pouring rain waiting to collect your child from swimming class. It's likely something that you'll refine over time, coming back to it again and again before you hit on something that feels right, exciting, and motivational.

Start with a simple phrase such as Jill's *"We empower thousands of people around the world to find and create more joy in their lives,"* and gently repeat and shape it over time until it feels as comfortable as an old pair of slippers. Then you've found your clarity of purpose, for the time being.

Jill's later progressed to: *"Our purpose is to gain huge satisfaction from empower thousands of people around the world to find and create more joy in their lives by helping others back to health."*

Your purpose will change over time, but stick with these comfy old slippers until they no longer feel right. Then start working on clarifying your purpose again – rinse and repeat. Remember, this is your *why* – not your *what* or your *how*. Make it meaningful and motivational.

INNOVATIVE APPROACH

One of the concepts you must accept in businesses is that the process never ends. There's always more to be done. Businesses are always evolving.

- You'll never have all of your marketing done.
- You'll never have all of your systems fully optimised.
- You'll never finish developing your customer experience.
- You'll never be in a position to know everything necessary to run the best practice possible.

You must be at peace with the fact that you and your business will forever evolve and move. There will come a time when you and your practice are no longer together, but whilst they are, you and it should and will continuously evolve.

Change is something that strikes fear into the heart of many people. But change is an essential element that will give your practice longevity. The following factors are always changing, and in turn they change the landscape of your business. Hence, they require you to change.

- Economic environment
- Technology
- Society and social constructs
- Your clinical sector
- Your patients' expectations
- Your internal business environment
- Your team

- The healthcare industry
- Your profession
- Treatment innovation

Because these things are ever-changing, both you and your practice also must be forever-changing – either to accommodate changes or move away from them. Over time, you'll find yourself in many unique situations compared to your fellow practitioners – situations that require you to evolve as a leader, manager, clinician, etc.

We are sure you've heard the phrase "evolve or die." This is what did it for the dinosaurs. They failed to evolve fast enough to keep up with their changing environment, and before long (relatively), they were extinct. The same goes for business. There are so many rapidly-evolving factors around us that impact us and our businesses. As business owners, we must do our best to keep pace with these changes or, like the dinosaurs, we'll suffer a slow, painful death.

Evolving requires you to change your products and services, how you price and promote them, how you treat and communicate with your patients, where and when you deliver your services – and your attitudes, beliefs, and thinking. This evolution can come in two ways: incremental changes, meaning small steps taken over longer periods of time, or through breakthrough improvements, which take place very quickly.

For years, healthcare has been evolving mostly through the incremental pattern of continuous improvement, with practice owners looking to implement changes slowly over several years. This approach is great, as it enables the logistics of change to be accommodated, not to mention the finances to be workable. This provides time for your team to adjust to new methods in a not-so-threatening way.

This continuous improvement was a management theory that came to the forefront after WW2 in Japan. A man by the name of William Edwards Deming, an American engineer, was brought into post-war Japan to help rejuvenate their crippled manufacturing industry (Deming 1981). In the post-war environment, there was neither time nor resources for large and innovative change. Deming refined a system which became a renowned cycle of continual improvement. Known as Kaizen, this method was made famous by Toyota. Using the principles, Toyota rose from being a small car producer to the largest automotive manufacturer in the world.

Do you have a Kaizen system in place that ensures reflection on your practice at least twice a year to identify potential improvements? This slow and steady approach to continuous improvement is a great tool, but it isn't always the best for the sustainability of businesses.

As we write this floor, the world is two years into the COVID pandemic. We have seen first-hand the need for rapid evolution of healthcare practices. Within weeks of restrictions being imposed, we saw thousands of healthcare practices taking their services online – selling products from their websites and conducting virtual consultations. This shift has changed the face of healthcare almost overnight. Those practices that haven't quickly innovated and embraced change have found themselves struggling to maintain momentum.

Remember our list of things that are constantly changing earlier on this floor? One factor that's always changing is our patients' expectations. With virtual consultations becoming the new norm for many, those practices which haven't developed their technical and clinical skills to deliver these online sessions will find themselves losing patients to more technically-advanced practices.

By the time you're reading this, you'll already know what the fallout from this has been, so you'll know if we were right!

THE NEED FOR CHANGE AND DISRUPTION

Without change, you'll become an extinct dinosaur. Like them, you don't get to dictate the speed of that change, which for many health-care practices can be a very uncomfortable reality. Uncertainty is something necessary to thrive, so hopefully you can see that change and innovation are good for you and the longevity of your practice.

Both the continuous improvement and rapid change models we've discussed are necessary to the success of your businesses, but they represent a reaction to external forces. However, there's another way to innovate, and that's to *be the change* and *disrupt your industry*. Instead of reacting to changes from outside your practice, you can create change inside that ripples out and shifts your industry.

Socrates is quoted as saying "The secret to change is to focus all of your energy not on fighting the old, but on building the new."
We'd like to tweak that slightly to say, "being the new."

Change is coming whether we like it or not. Why not be the force for change and create the transformation we want – rather than always fighting shifts brought by external forces?

Disruption by one person or an organisation which shakes up the direction and rate of change is well-documented in several industries. Just consider Richard Branson and the Virgin Airlines business, Anita Roddick and her Body Shop brand, or Elon Musk and his Tesla cars. They all shook industries to their core and drove others within their industries to change. Disruption can be a great thing in a well-established and conservative industry, like healthcare. If three people can initiate wholesale shifts in the way the airline, beauty, and automotive industries operate, absolutely you could shake up your profession or the healthcare sector. Are you reacting to external influences, or are you disrupting and *being the change*? Gandhi is commonly credited with saying:

"Be the change you want to see in the world."

You must stay motivated and excited about your business to create long-term success, being willing to change and if needed to shake up your industry. But how do you initiate such a change? Where do these new ideas come from? The answer is: listen. Listen to your own thoughts, feelings, and ideas as well as those of the people around you. Ideas are everywhere. Some are better than others but all of them deserve to be at least heard and considered before being acted upon or relegated to the "bad ideas" box.

Being open to doing things differently without feeling threatened or constrained can be hard. Many healthcare professionals come with historical baggage that holds them back, and many industries and specialties are governed by strict rules and legislation. But that doesn't mean change is impossible. Not many things are actually set in stone, especially in the face of well-thought-through and supported arguments for change. If change is needed to protect the longevity of your profession and businesses, then being a vector for that change is worth your effort. So how are you innovating in your practice? How are you supporting change? And how are you *being* the change?

EFFECTIVE STRATEGIES

What is a *business strategy*? Do you have one?

A business strategy is the combination of all the decisions and actions you take to achieve your business goals or vision and succeed in competitively positioning your business in your local market.

So it's your practice's working plan for how you will achieve your vision. It will help you prioritise your objectives, optimise your financial performance, and deliver an effective and sought-after patient experience. This is your master plan. There are lots of different ways to develop your strategy, but following are the most common approaches upon which you can build your internal processes and deliverables.

1. Cost-Leadership Strategy

This involves establishing yourself as the cheapest provider of a particular product or service in a given industry or geographical area. With this strategy, it is your job to reduce costs in every area in your practice in order to be competitive. This isn't a strategy we recommend to healthcare practitioners.

2. Differentiation Strategy

This involves setting out to be distinct from your competitors in some obvious ways. You could be an eco-based practice, minimising waste and using only ecologically-sound routines. Or you could be a high-end practice with top-notch décor, facilities, and clinical equipment. With this strategy, it's your job to create clear differentiators between you and your competitors.

3. Focus Strategy

This involves focusing your service delivery on a very narrow and clear segment of the local market. This could be specialising in specific pathologies or supporting people with specific demographics in some way, such as young athletes, those over fifty, etc. With this strategy, it's your job to clearly define a niche, establish that the niche as big enough to support your practice, then go all-in on developing a unique patient experience for that niche.

4. Creating-a-New-Market Strategy

This involves setting out to disrupt your industry by delivering either a totally new service or an established service in a way that has never been done before. In the medical world, there are often new discoveries or developments that would enable you to deliver a new service. But a physiotherapy practice that only delivers consultations virtually or a podiatry practice that only treats nail problems would be delivering established services in a new way.

5. Buying-the-Competition Strategy

This method is demonstrated well in the IT world where, for example, Facebook – who hardly ever develops their own new technologies – buys companies that have already done the development work. This isn't so common in the medical practice world, but hopefully you get the idea.

Are you intentionally following one of these strategies? If so, which strategy have you chosen? If you aren't, now is the time to realise that you must align your efforts to one of these strategies or another clearly-defined one. If your practice hasn't clearly defined which strategy you will develop, you will end up with a bland hybrid that makes delivering a thriving practice difficult.

That said, a vast majority of healthcare practices plump for strategy 2, most unwittingly – attempting to differentiate themselves in some way from the other local practices in their industry. Most do it very poorly. You can see evidence of this in your local area, with some very bland practices dotted up and down the high street and online – with no real clear differentiator between them.

When you choose your business strategy, you must commit and go all-in to do that strategy justice and maximise its potential. Consistently work your chosen strategy. Distil it down into systems that support your business development and move you towards your vision.

Educate your team on the strategy, so that they understand it and can help you deliver and improve on it – including spotting gaps and inefficiencies. Also, you must ensure that they have all the skills to work the business strategy and move towards your vision.

ORGANISATIONAL SYSTEMS

For a practice to have any longevity at all, it must include effective and efficient systems.

Systems are documented, tried, and tested ways of delivering a repeated business task to minimise wastage and ensure efficiency and consistency. Systems maximise your use of time and increase productivity. They also minimise the decisions you must make – and with the possibility of decision fatigue (a well-documented negative effect on your mental capacity) – systems must be an all-round good thing. Business systems and the processes within them are the signposts and blueprint for running your business day-to-day. Good systems enable each business to do their best with the resources they have. Having effective and efficient systems in place enables practices to:

- Deliver smooth customer service
- Improve their processes
- Delivery a consistent and high-quality patient experience
- Improve employee performance
- Utilise resources more efficiently
- Reduce costs
- Grow in a controlled way
- Recruit the best team members

Your systems will always be evolving, so there will always be room for improvement, but they should be as good as they can be with the resources you currently have. The core systems every practice should have in place are:

- **Finance systems** – to stay current and proactive with your money
- **Patient management systems** – including booking and onboarding
- **Clinical systems** – to ensure consistent clinical service delivery
- **Human resource systems** – to ensure good team management
- **Marketing systems** – to consistently attract new patients and support existing ones in their relationship with you
- **Facilities and equipment management systems** – to maximise utilisation, longevity, and impact
- **Business administration systems** – to make sure everything runs smoothly

Just a little warning – it isn't sufficient just to have some systems in place. To ensure your business longevity, you must have effective and efficient systems across the board.

"94 percent of problems in businesses are systems driven, only 6 percent are people driven."
William Edwards Deming (Boardman 1994)

There's an irony that you need a system for creating and evaluating your systems!

EXERCISE
How to Develop a System

We would like to take you through a super simple system to help you develop effective practice systems.

STEP 1: Identify Your Problem
If you're looking for areas of your business to systematise, think about:
- Tasks that are done frequently or repeatedly over time
- Complex tasks that take a lot of time to complete

- Bottlenecks or things that frustrate you in your business
- Areas of the business you don't want to be involved with

Which of these triggers an idea? That would be a great place to start with setting up a new system in your business.

STEP 2: Plan Out the Process

Document every step of a process that will help you overcome your problem. A top tip for this step is to write each step on a separate piece of paper, so that you can reorder the sequence as you go through and see gaps or flaws in the process flow. Once you have the steps in place, create a digital document of all the steps.

STEP3: Your Dummy Run

This is where you go through the system for the first time. You can do this alone if it will be your job, or do it alongside someone else if it will be part of their role. Step by step, go through the process and update the document anywhere the wording of the process is unclear or inaccurate. For example, work on your new patient welcome and first appointment processes. Or the process for monitoring stock levels and reordering when levels get low. What are the step-by-step systems to support both of these scenarios, so that in the future, they will always be carried out in exactly the same way – ensuring that nothing is missed?

STEP 4: Try It for Real

This is where you set about using your newly-documented system *for real*. Whoever is responsible for the system takes it on and uses it in real-time. Once it's being used, other issues may crop up that need remedying. Make sure whoever is responsible to make further changes to the document as they work through it is enabled to make the system as good as it can be.

STEP 5: Diary a Review

Set a date six months in the future to gather everyone on your team and review the systems they use within your practice. This should ensure that all of your systems are as up-to-date and effective as possible. It also gives you an opportunity to discuss new systems that need setting up.

If this is your first foray into business systems, or you had only previously dabbled in optimising them, you'll soon see that once you start using effective and efficient business systems, there's no going back. You'll wonder how on earth you managed before.

Do you have systems in place for processes that get repeated many times in a year?

Do you have systems in place to help you deliver a consistent patient experience?

Do you have systems in place to make sure everyone can do their tasks as efficiently and effectively as possible?

EFFECTIVE USE OF RESOURCES

The resources in your practice fall into four main categories:

- People
- Physical resources
- Money
- Time

Using all of these optimally is a key part of building a business with longevity.

YOUR PEOPLE

Everyone in your profession – and therefore all of your local competitors – may have similar qualifications, skills, equipment, and services on offer. The thing that cannot be replicated – and therefore the thing that differentiates your practice – is the people.

We're all individuals. We all have a unique combination of experiences, talents, beliefs, passions, ideas, and drivers. The main factor that will differentiate your practice is your team. These people play a big part in your competitive advantage. So recruiting, training, and retaining good people is essential to your business success and longevity.

Your job therefore is to tap into all the unique traits your team brings with them to differentiate your practice locally, as well as maximise your use of their clinical and personal skills, personalities, and new ideas. This is important for two reasons. First, to enable you to deliver a highly unique patient experience. But second, because besides your team meeting your business needs, you also must meet their individual employment and career needs in order to nurture and retain them. You must know what people desire in relation to their careers and working lives, so that you can support and give them these desires. Doing so will optimise their contribution to the practice, while fulfilling their professional and personal aspirations.

Talking with your team about career progression is essential. But what is more important is actually listening to what they say and working hard to support them in their career and work/life aspirations. Yes, there's a chance they may take what you teach them and go elsewhere. But it's an amazing feeling to help others find happiness, and if they move on, they open the door for another unique individual to join your team and make an impact.

You must keep motivating, inspiring, and rewarding your team and yourself (in all of this, don't forget yourself – you have needs that must be met too) to keep everyone happy and thriving.

Motivation can look different to each person but could include:

- **Empowerment** – people thrive when they are trusted and enabled to do the job in a way that works well for them and the practice.
- **Goal Setting** – goals of all shapes and sizes can really help motivate people if you target them accurately (not everyone is driven by money).
- **Stretching** – some people respond well to being challenged to raise their game by developing new clinical skills or new knowledge.
- **Bigger Responsibilities** – being trusted can provide a huge boost in motivation.

To inspire your team, you can:

- Show people what is possible by spotlighting examples inside and outside your industry.
- Share quotes, inspiring videos, or stories.
- Provide exposure to role models who can act as mentors.
- Seek advice or inspiration from those on your team.
- Provide time away for volunteering.
- Rewards come in many forms, including:
- Financial bonuses or pay rises
- Little notes of thanks
- Public praise
- Performance awards for work-related acts of kindness
- Meaningful and relevant gifts (avoid the obvious options of chocolates, flowers, or beer)
- Paid leave
- Equipment or facilities upgrades.

Invest in your people, develop them, provide genuine career progression, reward them, retain them, and get them delivering a high-quality service. That's how to maximise the impact of your people resources.

YOUR PHYSICAL RESOURCES

It goes without saying (we hope) that maximising your physical resources is crucial to building a strong long-lasting business. Doing this effectively will often come down to the systems you have in place – which we've already covered on this floor – but here are a few other pointers to help you maximise your equipment, consumables, digital resources, and physical space:

Using Your Physical Space

Making the most of physical space means maximising the value you derive from your building. To do this effectively and efficiently you must be clear on the potential value-based uses of the individual spaces you have. Whether that is consultation, assessment, treatment, education, or hospitality space. You then need to equip your spaces to maximise their potential, as well as effectively schedule the use of those spaces to maximise their value.

> What spaces do you have?
> Are they equipped to best effect?
> Are they used to their maximum effect?

Controlling your stock

Minimising wastage and lost opportunities to sell stock and maximising the potential to fully treat every patient attending your practice requires you to have a clear understanding of stock levels, expiry dates, and predicted usage rates. It also requires you to be purchasing the right products and stock items in the first place, as well as structuring your treatment pathways to use all of the relevant products effectively.

> Are you monitoring stock?
> Do you actively sell products to all relevant patients?
> Have you built product use into your treatment plans?

Maximising Usage of Technical Equipment

Technical equipment is usually a big capital cost to the business, so maximising its use is important. This includes maximising the potential of both clinical and administrative support equipment. A key with this is making sure that you and your team are trained in using the equipment you have, so that you can maximise its impact. Sometimes with clinical equipment, maximising its potential will require you to attract a cohort of patients with specific pathologies. This will also require your marketing to be up to scratch.

Are you using all your equipment to its maximum?
Is everyone trained to use the equipment relevant to their role?
Are you attracting enough of the right patients to maximise clinical equipment use?

YOUR FINANCIAL RESOURCES

The key objectives of most businesses is to serve their customers while making a profit. Making a profit requires you to be a good custodian of your financial resources. You must make money and spend it wisely. Proactively managing your business finances helps you build a stable business with longevity.

Financial resources start with a solid income, and that comes from good marketing (which we covered on Floor 4) and effective pricing. This will give you more financial resources to work with.

Pricing

Many healthcare practices under-price their services, basing them on what their competitors are doing and what they feel their patients can or will be prepared to pay. Pricing must start with knowing your costs.

EXERCISE
Minimum Patient Fee

This isn't an all-encompassing exercise, but it should help you start getting to grips with your pricing by using some average numbers. Follow these steps:

STEP 1: Calculate how many weeks per year you want your practice working.

STEP 2: Confirm your annual running costs, including your personnel costs and a salary for you.

STEP 3: Calculate what you want to add to that as a percentage for a security buffer, savings, and profit. This will give you your total costs.

STEP 4: Divide your total costs by your working weeks to get your average weekly cost.

STEP 5: Considering a good month and a not-so-good month, calculate the average number of patient appointments filled per week.

STEP 6: Divide your average weekly total costs by the average number of filled appointments.

STEP 7: What is your average minimum patient appointment fee?

This assumes no other products or services are being sold at a profit. It gives you the baseline for all of your pricing. More complex and demanding appointments will be charged at more than this, but no appointment should be charged at less than this.

Once you've got your pricing sorted next you need to be controlling your expenses.

Expenses

The costs of running your practice are controlled by market forces to an extent. The price for things like professional registration and insurance, property rent, or purchases of large capital items are highly influenced by external market forces. You have more control over personnel costs, outfitting expenses, and technology investments etc. With these expenses, you can negotiate and choose from more market options.

Your expenses can be influenced in a downward direction by your spending habits, purchasing choices, and negotiation skills.

Your Numbers

The third element of managing your financial resources is to know the rest of your numbers and how they all interact. You must know them well and monitor them constantly. Every week you should be monitoring:

- Cashflow
- Net income
- Expenses
- Profit and loss
- Gross profit

You're looking for sharp spikes, upward or downward trends, or any patterns that will give you the information to make different decisions and strengthen the financial position inside the business. Solid pricing, purchasing control, and financial monitoring will help with managing your financial resources to the maximum.

How solid is your pricing?
How controlled is your spending?
Are you reviewing your numbers every week?

YOUR TIME RESOURCES

Time is a level playing field. It's a resource we all have the same amount of and almost universally need more of, but it's something that can very easily be wasted or not utilised fully. Good time management really comes down to two things in your practice:

1. Effective systems and processes
2. Discipline

Systems and Processes

How well you utilise your clinical and administration time comes down to the systems and processes you have in place (or the lack of them) and how well you adhere to them. The biggest wins to be had here are the introduction of effective systems, processes, and technology-based digitisation and automations to support them. We've already covered systems on this floor, so let's focus on technology.

Technology, if you use it properly, can provide you with lots of time-saving opportunities. Things that you can digitise or automate in your practice may include:

- Patient review and appointment reminders
- Patient note-taking
- Recall e-mails
- Blog writing and posting
- Letter writing
- Social media scheduling
- Requests for feedback and reviews
- Thank you and reward letter writing and sending
- Missed appointment notices and billing
- Financial reporting
- Website analytics reporting
- Delivering team training
- New patient pack delivery

Using technology in this way can help you improve consistency, increase efficiency, and optimise the patient experience. With more purpose-built digital practice management systems on the market, many of these tasks are genuinely only a few clicks away from being completed. With a combination of easily available digital dictation, practice management software, and third-party apps, many of these tasks are genuinely only a few clicks and a few minutes away from being completed.

Discipline

"Discipline is the bridge between goals and accomplishment."
(Jim Rohn n.d.)

Utilising time well in your practice is hugely reliant on discipline – both yours and that of your team members. This includes discipline to stick to the established systems and processes, such as completing tasks in the most efficient way. It also includes discipline to get on with the necessary work without distractions.

One type of discipline is entirely the responsibility of the leadership within the practice. Owners and senior practice managers must lead by example – which includes policing systems implementation and correcting behaviour where needed. As a combination, this will result in good practice discipline.

The other type of discipline is a whole other book! Time management training can only take you so far. A discipline to work efficiently is driven by our beliefs, attitude, and drivers. If either you or any of your team members struggle with this, then there's work to be done on personal development and time management. But having the awareness that part of the problem is discipline is a great starting point.

POSITIVE CULTURE

Organisational culture was first discussed by Dr. Elliott Jaques in his book *The Changing Culture of a Factory* (Jaques 1952). It really came to mass awareness during the mid to late 1990s when organisations like Google rewrote the book on how businesses behave and how they treat their employees. Since then, businesses like Zappos, L.L. Bean, and TOMS have focused heavily on developing internal cultures that foster and reward creativity, collaboration, and innovation.

With local and national business awards like "Fortune's 100 Best Companies to Work For" now being popular, company culture has become a big part of what it means to create a successful and sustainable business.

So, what do we mean by business culture? According to Wikipedia, a business culture: "encompasses values and behaviours that contribute to the unique social and psychological environment of a business…It represents the collective values, beliefs, and principles of organizational members."

In short, culture is the personality or soul of your business, reflecting the values by which it operates.

You may never have considered the fact that your practice has an internal culture, but whether you see it or not, every organisation involving more than one person has some kind of culture. Those cultures can be healthy, but they can also be unhealthy, so just having a culture isn't enough. Yours must be a positive, authentic one to achieve your vision while fostering happiness and building lasting patient relationships.

We've all experienced or heard of organisations where the culture is unhealthy or toxic, perhaps based on fear, intimidation, meanness, or bullying. Some cultures aren't authentically aligned to the owner or ethos of the business, so operations feel forced and false. These aren't the kind of cultures you want to establish and nurture.

Throw a random group of people together – for example, your team – and a culture will develop naturally. But much like growing prize flowers rather than weeds in your garden, you don't want to leave it to random birds and winds to bring your seeds. You must be very intentional about planting and nurturing specific cultural seeds. Setting boundaries, celebrating certain behaviours, and encouraging openness and honesty will all help you develop a culture with specific elements.

To ensure longevity of your practice, you must intentionally build a culture that is healthy, positive, and supportive of everyone involved in the business. This takes time and energy, but there are very definite rewards to doing this. Positive, healthy organisational cultures can help with:

- **Recruiting the best team members** – your reputation will attract talent.
- **Retaining employees** – people won't want to leave.
- **Building a community of happy patients** – they will feel like they belong to something.
- **Improved customer satisfaction** – patients will love being in such a positive, happy place.
- **Better decision-making** – decisions are made based on a clear understanding of what you're aiming for.
- **Raised business profile** – people talk about remarkable businesses.
- **Healthier team members** – people will experience lower stress levels and a happier working environment.
- **Increased revenue** – a happy organisation ripples out, attracting more business opportunities
- **Increased employee engagement** – people love being part of something they believe in.

Investing time, energy, and money into developing your own organisational culture can really reap rewards for you in your practice. You don't have to be a huge organisation with a big budget and a large HR team to be intentional about building a business culture. If you understand why having a good one is important, that's a great starting point.

Don't be mistaken into thinking that this is just about coloured bean bags, free coffee, and a ping-pong table. A businesses culture runs much deeper than that. Your practice culture should really be rooted in the core values that are important to you and embedded in how you do business. These aren't just words they need to really guide how you work.

Just to refresh you:

Drivers – are emotional things that really motivate us – the things that can help build a happy life (see Floor 3).

Values – are principles and beliefs that we hold true and must live and work by to feel aligned with what we're doing – in short, the rules we follow when no one is looking. Your core values should reflect where you are now but also where you aspire to be.

To go back to Jill's business example, the values that she and her team have agreed to strive for are:

- Happiness trumps every other card.
- Honesty comes a close second.
- Everything can be figured out.
- Living your dreams is compulsory.
- Everyone is your equal.
- More listening, less talking.
- Celebrate success, no matter how small.

So, to set about intentionally creating your practice culture, you must start with your values. Can you identify your practice core values?

EXERCISE
Understanding Core Values

Here is a simple exercise to help you understand core values you want to demonstrate in your practice.

Get your team together with a cup of tea, a blank sheet of paper per person, and a pair of scissors. You're going to flesh out what is important to you as a team. Deciding what is important and not important in your practice ensures that your core values are relevant and effective for you. Ask each team member to write down their answers to the following questions on a fresh line of their paper:

1. *What are the top three qualities in a practice team member?*
2. *What three personal or practice-wide traits would be detrimental to the success of the practice?*
3. *What three ways of working within the practice will support success and personal development?*

Now cut each answer out and stack them into piles, so you have all the answers to Q1 in one pile, etc. Working through each pile, create a concise list of everything, combining some responses to remove any duplication. Then with all the collated answers for each question, see if you can identify two or three clear favourites. These, for now, can be your core values. Use these to help decision-making, reinforce behaviour, etc. Doing this will nurture a culture that supports your practice – making it a place where your employees feel they can thrive.

Once you're clear on your values, you can start building a picture of what your culture will look like. This will include a combination of things that come to mind when you review your values, purpose, vision, and mission. A simple question to ask yourself here is: *How do I want my team, patients, referrers, collaborators, suppliers, and myself to feel about our practice?*

Once you start to paint a picture of what that culture looks like, the next step is to look at where you are now in relation to that picture, then identify areas that must change in order for this culture to be a reality. The simple question to ask yourself around achieving your desired culture is: *What needs to change?*

The next step is to share your ideas around the culture you want to develop, and decide what needs to change. Discuss this with your team and get their input. It's really important that this is a collaboration and not something you impose on your team. The two questions to ask here are: *Are we all in agreement?* and *How do we start to make this happen?*

Once you have a consensus of opinion and some ideas for how to make it happen, you can set about embedding the culture you want into your organisation. This will take time, but if you're all clear on what you're aiming for and what needs to be done, you can start to make it happen.

There may be some difficult conversations along the way, if some of your team members aren't in tune with the values you identify as core to your practice. This may lead some existing team members to question if they still want to be part of this business. Don't be afraid of this, as it could well be a good thing. Helping team members to see more clearly if they fit or not – potentially hence deciding to leave – will help you build a stronger team in the long-term. On the flip side, having a clear culture will make it easier to recruit the right people in the future. You'll be able to see very clearly if someone is a fit for your business or not.

In any organisation, there can often be resistance to change. But hopefully with everyone on board during the ideas phase – and the fact that this is actually designed to support everyone – you should be able to make changes without too many tantrums. During this process, it's also a great idea to make culture a standing item in your regular team meetings, so that it stays prominent in people's minds and reinforces its importance to your future success.

So please don't tag culture as trendy business-speak or attempt to build a culture by merely installing a fridge full of doughnuts. Dedicating time and attention to working on developing a real business culture that will serve you now, and in the future, will not be a waste of resources.

YOUR ONGOING SUCCESS AND HAPPINESS

Hopefully this final floor has given you some food for thought and encouraged you to start thinking about your exit strategy and building a really robust business that will last and thrive for as long as you intend it to while making you happy to boot.

None of this will happen by accident. All of these elements that can contribute to a thriving, long-lasting business will require a clear vision and decisive action in order to make this a reality. But now, at least, you have the insight into what is required – whether you want your business to be here for five or one thousand years.

ACTION POINTS TO ENSURE YOU ARE ETERNISED

☐ Complete Identifying Personal Drives and The Achievement Jar exercises

☐ Have clarity of purpose and know that your business will forever evolve, appreciating the need for change and disruption

☐ Identify your business strategy

☐ Complete How to Develop a System exercise

☐ Keep motivating, inspiring and rewarding your team

☐ Use your resources

☐ Complete Minimum Patient Fee exercise

☐ Embrace a positive culture

☐ Complete Understanding Core Values exercise

YOU'RE NOW ETERNISED √

NOTES

ELEVATE:
The Complete Process

J & J x

We hope that this book has helped you elevate your thinking around your practice and what is possible for both you and it. We also hope that it has allowed you to really focus on the two important elements – success and happiness – that don't often sit side-by-side in business books.

At the beginning of our book, we looked at the definitions for the word *elevate*:

1. to move or raise to a higher place or position; lift up
2. to raise to a higher state, rank, or office; exalt; promote
3. to raise to a higher intellectual or spiritual level
4. to raise the spirits; put in high spirits
5. to raise (the voice) in pitch or volume

You've hopefully completed all seven floors (chapters) to help you through the process of elevating you and your business.

We hope you're now in a position to bring to life more quickly and effectively the practice you dream of owning. Our ultimate aim is to equip you in better serving your patients, without sacrificing your own wants and needs.

We want to wish you well in your practice development adventures. We truly hope you enjoy the journey and the joy and rewards it brings. Thank you for allowing us to be part of this amazing journey.

Jill and Jonathan

ACTION POINTS TO ENSURE YOU ARE ELEVATED

☐ Be Energised

☐ Let Go

☐ Engage

☐ Know Your Value

☐ Take Action

☐ Transform

☐ Be Eternised

YOU'RE NOW ELEVATED √

REFERENCES

n.d. https://www.guinnessworldrecords.com/world-records/oldesthotel.

Boardman, Thomas J. 1994. "The statistician who changed the world: W. Edwards Deming, 1900-1993." *The American Statistician 48, no. 3* 179-187.

Covey, Stephen R. 1989. *The 7 habits of highly successful people.* NewYork: Fireside.

Craig Davis. n.d. https://quotecatalog.com/communicator/craig-davis.

Deming, William Edwards. 1981. "Improvement of quality and productivity through action by management." *National productivity review 1, no. 1* 12-22.

n.d. *https://www.solutionreach.com/rethinking-the-patient-providerrelationship.* https://www.solutionreach.com/rethinking-thepatient-provider-relationship.

Jaques, Elliott. 1952. *The changing culture of a factory.*

Kratochvíl, Martin. 2012. *The Development of a Succession Planning Strategy for a Family-owned Business.*

Napoleon Hill. n.d. https://www.brainyquote.com/authors/napoleonhill-quotes.

Robbins, Tony. 2008. *Unlimited power: The new science of personal achievement.* Simon and Schuster.

Rohn, Jim. n.d. *10 unforgettable quotes by Jim Rohn.* Accessed 2022. https://www.success.com/10-unforgettable-quotes-by-jim-rohn/.

Sone, Hidekazu. 2013. "Tradition and Innovation in Japanese Long-Established Companies: Focus on E-Business." *Seventh International Conference of Innovative Mobile and Internet Services in Ubiquitous Computing.* IEEE. 739-742.

Van Kleeck, Gail. 1999. *How You See Anything Is How You See Everything: A Treasury of Simple Wisdom.* Andrews McMeel Publishing.

Printed in Great Britain
by Amazon